SHEFFIELD LAD

SHEFFIELD LAD

a memoir

growing up in Sheffield
in the 1940s and 1950s

JOHN FOSTER

All rights reserved

© John Foster, 2021

ISBN: 9798753087874

Cover image is a painting of the author as a child

by Kate Rose

For my children

my children's children

and their children's children

As you set out for Ithaca
Hope your road is a long one,
Full of adventure, full of discovery...

Keep Ithaca always in your mind,
Arriving there is what you're destined for.
But don't hurry the journey at all.
Better if it lasts for years,
So you're old by the time you reach the island,
Wealthy with all you've gained on the way,
Not expecting Ithaca to make you rich.

Ithaca gave you the marvellous journey.
Without her you wouldn't have set out.
She has nothing left to give you now.

And if you find her poor, Ithaca won't have fooled you.
Wise as you have become, so full of experience,
You'll have understood by then what these Ithacas mean.

from **Ithaca**
C.P. Cavafy

Contents

I	Origins	1
II	My Dad, flicks, football and fantasy	9
III	Early days	26
IV	16 Northcote Road: at home with Mum	33
V	Shopping with Mum	53
VI	Sundays	67
VII	School days: Carfield	75
VIII	School days: King Ted's	101
IX	Teenage years: St Valentine and St Silas	131
X	Feast days and fun days	145
XI	Grandma and dialect	171
XII	Holiday jobs	177
	Postscript	187
	Other books by John Foster	189

Foreword

Monday, February 22, 2021.

Yesterday I visited my old boyhood haunts. Feeling stir crazy in this eternal Covid lockdown and in search of exercise somewhere different, I had set off driving aimlessly and found myself homing in, as if on autopilot, on the place where I lived as a boy, from 1940 until 1958, when I left for university. I parked my car outside the Church of the Nazarene – what used to be St Peter's Mission Church in my day – opposite where my family home once stood. My part of Northcote Road has changed. The unbroken rows of terraced houses have disappeared, along with the cobblestones, replaced mostly by a row of undistinguished, squat bungalows, an ugliness only relieved by a handful of prettier houses in the distance.

The street seems wider too. Only the red-brick rear aspect of the church lends it a familiar feel. Of the Memorial Hall which stood alongside the church there remains no trace, except for the steep brick steps leading up to a blank wall where its entrance used to be. The church has moved up in the world since my day and has assumed a businesslike air. The brickwork is spruced up and the roof is new. A notice board proudly proclaims not only its own vicar, the Reverend Tim Burton no less, but also an official contact person for the hire of rooms.

Behind me, my school building lies in ruins, newly demolished in the interests of public safety. Eerily for 2021, there are no other cars parked on Northcote Road, almost as if we were back in 1940. It is surprisingly easy to conjure them all up from this empty street: Mrs Ashby, Jack Warris, Tom and Rina Kendall, Mrs Woodhouse, Miffer, Charlie Finch, Grandma.

And Mum and Dad, who made me and all my memories.

†

I Origins

I used to lie in bed thinking about topics that I could address to players that would have an impact on them. I would talk about miners, shipyard workers, welders, tool manufacturers, you know, people who come of poor origins. I used to ask them what did your grandfather do? what did your father do? I have to get the feeling inside of them that what their grandfathers and their grandmothers worked for is part of them, and they have to display that meaning. It's a fact of life that where we come from is important - you come out with an identity. I come from Govan. I'm a Govan boy.

Alex Ferguson, football coach

I come from Sheffield. I'm a Sheffield lad.

I was born in Nether Edge Hospital in the first January of the Second World War, one of the coldest months on record and the snowiest to boot. It was a few days after food rationing was introduced.

Ice floes were reported on the Thames and, on the 26th of January 1940, 120 centimetres of snow fell on our city. When my mother brought me home, at three weeks old, the snow was already piled up to the window sill of our house on Northcote Road. A cold welcome to a warm-hearted city!

I was born with my right foot facing backwards, and, urged on by the midwife and the neonatal paediatrician, my mother spent long hours every day for the whole of my first year massaging my ankle to persuade my foot to point in the right direction. Her tender maternal therapy was successful, and I thank her for it. For many weeks of this first year my face and much of my body were painted blue, as I had developed severe impetigo, which needed prolonged treatment with gentian violet. In my second year I acquired my trademark 'Spitfire' scar in the centre of my forehead by tumbling forward and colliding with the corner of the fender. In my early passports, the Spitfire appears as my 'distinguishing feature', although it's now faded to such an extent that it's hardly noticeable.

When my mother died in 1989, I realised how little I knew of my parents' world, when they were small, when they were young and full of hope, how they had felt, what they had hoped for. Now I regret that I didn't ask those questions. Now I can only tell what little I do know.

Dad was born on 6th January, 1906. His family lived in Carter Place, in Heeley. His sister Kate was the eldest in the family; then came Albert, then my father, Leonard, followed by Arthur, and finally Louisa. Schooling was not compulsory until the Fisher Act of 1918, barely a year before Dad reached the new school leaving age, 14. Young Len Foster spent much of this his fourteenth year avoiding the 'school bobby'. Like many 13-year-olds, he didn't see the point of school. He had managed well enough without it so far.

left Dad at 14 or 15, right Mum at 16

Len suffered from rheumatic fever in his late teens, and his parents were informed that he would not live beyond thirty. That, I am embarrassed to confess, is all I know about my dad's childhood. And that is a damned shame. I probably thought it didn't matter. But it does.

Mum, Nellie Billard, was born on 22nd September, 1909. At least, I think she was. She was never quite sure. Until she left school, she had always celebrated her birthday on 22nd October, but at that point she had to obtain a birth certificate to arrange documents for employment purposes. Her birth certificate begged to differ, placing her date of birth one month earlier. Mum suspected that Grandma had quite possibly mixed up the dates when she was registered, as, like the old woman who lived in a shoe, she had so many children she didn't know what to do. Grandma may well have become 'mithered' by the paperwork, her large family and sickly husband, and confused the dates. Life was hard.

My grandma, also Nellie, was the daughter of John Clarke, a labourer, and his wife Sarah, both illiterate. She had six children by her first husband, Henry Billard, the son of a chimney sweep. Alice was the oldest sibling, born in the 19th century and almost a decade older than Mum, but was of little help around the house to Grandma, being not only partially sighted but also totally lacking in domestic skills. In between were brothers Tom, Harry and John, with younger sister Lily, two or three years junior to Mum. Anyone with an ounce of knowledge about how families were run in the early 20th century will realise that this left young Nellie with considerable domestic duties. She became the little mother around the house. Although she was clever at school, she was obliged to leave as soon as possible to take up work in a factory. Every little helped in the household economy. She found a job at Skelton's in Heeley Bottom, as an unskilled or semi-skilled worker, polishing and assembling garden tools. Her dream job would have been secretarial work in an office, the height of ambition for a girl of her class in post-Great War Heeley, but even this modest aspiration was unattainable, as it required a further year's schooling.

Grandma was widowed before she was 30, and was left with six children. They lived in a small terraced house, two up two down, at number 10 Northcote Road.

Left Grandma widowed for the first time, right her mother, Sarah Clarke

The womenfolk shared the two bedrooms, while the boys shared the attic. Grandma found to her chagrin that she just could not cope, could not feed all these mouths. Two of the boys, John and Harry, the ones she judged would stand up best to the experience, were sacrificed to live in the orphanage, for two years, until Harry was old enough to go out to work. Mum told me that it was heart-breaking for Grandma, but that she felt she had no choice if they were all to survive. Subsequently, she married again, to a widower, Fred Price, shovel-maker, joining up with another ready-made family, some of them already grown-up. She was now Nellie Price, the mother of ten or eleven children. God knows where they all slept! Into this second marriage was born Annie, a new little sister for my mother to nurture. The two became very close and remained so throughout their lives.

Annie's birthdate is as unclear as my mother's. My cousin Geoff, her son, told me: 'Her birth certificate says 13th April [1916], but she always used the 30th as her birthday. The story goes that the registrar was deaf and entered the wrong date on the certificate. But as he was an important man in a big office, no correction was sought for fear of being admonished, and what did it matter anyhow?'

There were indeed more important things to worry about. Before long, Nellie Price was widowed for a second time.

The link between Mum and Dad was my Uncle Harry, who was a similar age to Dad. Uncle Harry, a kind and patient man, a man with a sharp mind, who always beat me at chess, who gave me his own chess set and board.

Len and Harry were the dynamic midfield duo of Ann's Road FC, the marginally less cultured Heeley equivalent of the Barry Bannon – Kieran Lee axis[1], fiery, muck and bullets lads with basin haircuts and the occasional touch of sheer class. Allegedly. Len was still living with his parents in Carter Place, not far away. His elder sister, Kate, and his two brothers, Albert and Arthur, had already left home and married. Len and Nellie had been 'courting' for about three years, when the news broke that the house at number 16 was soon to become empty and available to rent at nine shillings and a penny per week. That sounds very little, but the average weekly wages of a working man were around £2, and in any case Dad was currently out of work and had no

Harry Billard

---

[1] *Don Revie likened them to Giles and Bremner, whereas I understand that Sir Alex is more inclined to compare them to Scholes and Butt.*

Ann's Rd FC
Dad front row, Harry back row, both 2nd from right

prospects of employment. The owner was a certain Mrs Hastings, who was also Grandma's landlady. Mum begged Mrs Hastings to keep the house for her and Dad, which, bless her, she did. Nellie and Len married on Easter Monday, 1937, with a Wilkins Micawber-like faith that something would turn up. As feared, Nellie was obliged to give up her job at Skelton's immediately, as married women were not allowed to be employed at the factory[2]. It was considered to be taking a man's job. It was not an auspicious beginning to married life, but Harry helped them to buy a little second-hand furniture, and some kind soul gave them a bed. It is unclear how they paid the first week's rent, but Dame Fortune and Mrs Hastings smiled on them, Len soon gained employment as a grinder, and Nellie used all her survival skills and domestic economics expertise to eke out a modest living.

---

[2] *It is worth remembering that such practice was common, and until 1946 any woman civil servant was obliged to resign from her post upon marrying. In the Foreign Service this rule was in place until 1973.*

Dad was already 31 when they married, and Mum 28. I think I can imagine the conversation:

'This could be our last chance, Len. If we don't take number 16, when are we ever going to get somewhere?'
'It's all reight thee saying that, lass, but how will we pay t' rent?'
'We'll manage, or we'll just have to live with my mother.'
'Reight enough, then, lass, reight enough.'

The risks we take for love! I thank my lucky stars that these two fools were brave enough to rush in where angels feared to tread.

wedding day

Mum on doorstep of new home

II My Dad, flicks, football and fantasy

The first time I remember seeing Dad at work was at Smith's Wheel at the foot of Furnival Street. I had gone there with Mum, in 1943 or 1944, to take Dad his packing-up, wrapped in a page from the Star. We watched from the doorway, with me trying to pick him out from all the similar men in weskits and flat caps, all with a muffler or a mask over their mouth and nose. Mum pointed him out, at the centre, the very hub of it all, sending out shower upon shower of the most beautiful gold and silver sparks, a magical display that I have never forgotten. He was sharpening table knives, his proud Sheffield craft, and he was rated, I learned later, among the very best at his trade. He was no 'little mester', no forger and maker of blades, merely an archetypal Sheffield grinder, the salt of the Steel City's earth. From then on, I snatched every opportunity to see Dad 'making sparks', as did my younger cousin Geoff. He still to this day enthuses about his visits to Uncle Len's wheel.

Later, Dad would have to compromise his craft, as our cutlery industry hit the buffers in competition with cheap Far Eastern products, and would take up heavier work, for instance grinding machetes, axes, and agricultural blades. This was at a time when his health was suffering in the last few years of his life.

Blade grinding was filthy, damp work. The grinder sat astride a wooden saddle, behind the grindstone, which turned at frightening speed, driven by belts connected by a series of cogs and crankshafts to the main drive wheel. The speed of the grindstone was not under the control of the grinder. It was lubricated by water picked up from a trough, and so the grinder was subjected to a constant fine spray, which itself was contaminated by particles of dirt and steel filings. Strictly speaking, the grinder should have worn goggles to protect his eyes, but this was impractical, as he soon was blinded by the spray and the muck thrown onto the goggles by the grindstone. Consequently, some of the metal filings which were ground from the blade found their way into my dad's eyes. At home, hanging by the side of the strop[3], was a large horseshoe magnet with sewing needles clinging to it. These needles were what my mum used on a regular basis to remove the 'moits'[4] embedded my dad's cornea, using a steady hand, a keen eye, and the acquired magnetic power of the needle. She often had to use these needles to tease spells[5] out of my finger before they went septic. In the case of a stubbornly embedded moit, Dad had to take a bus to the hospital for expert treatment.

In the late 1940s, Dad's employers had decided it would be beneficial to pay their workers on a piecework basis, and he was to all intents and purposes self-employed. He recorded his work in a small note-book, along with the rate per piece or per hundred pieces. Largely owing to his lack of schooling, dad's arithmetic was not strong, and I was allotted the job of working out the multiplication sums and the totals at the foot of the page. All this was done with a stubby pencil, and the note-book, although still very neatly organised, soon became dog-eared and grubby. Looking back, I wonder if Mum checked my arithmetic. It seems too important to have left to an eight-year-old. Dad did have a ready reckoner, a small handbook which did multiplications

---

[3] *For more on the strop, see the Chapter IV*

[4] *The word moit must be a local or trade expression, as it is not defined in dictionaries as having this meaning – a steel filing embedded in the eye of a grinder. It probably derives from the biblical word mote, meaning a speck of dust or dirt. It may also be simply mote spoken with a Sheffield accent. After all, hole is pronounced oil, and 'put t' wood in t' oil' is the Sheffield version of 'close the door, please'.*

[5] *Spells were splinters of wood under the skin, very often dirty, as I'd picked them up in the woods.*

and divisions for you, a sort of pre-digital calculator, but he preferred to entrust his weekly wages to me, which made me feel proud and important. I did not think any the less of him for this. He was my dad.

Eventually, in the early 1950s, the company that contracted some of its work out to Dad folded, citing inability to compete with cheap Far Eastern imports, and he was out of work for a spell. Eventually, he found a job with a firm on Saxon Road, near Heeley Bridge. In the mid-1950s the firm moved to Chesterfield, and Dad moved with them, which meant a long daily bus ride to work, but he was happy to still have a job.

As well as his 40 hours plus at the grindstone, Dad worked at a sizeable allotment in Arbourthorne, about a mile from home. There he had a large greenhouse and an extensive plot of land for growing vegetables. As a gardener, Dad was nothing less than a genius. He produced a huge crop of delicious tomatoes every summer, far too many for us to eat, and some of which we were able to sell. The rest Mum bottled for the winter or made into chutney. Onions, potatoes, carrots, turnips, cabbage, runner beans, peas, cauliflowers and lettuce were plentiful, and of course were organic, although we had no inkling of the benefits of organic food at the time. Dad used manure because it was available and it worked. We had rhubarb, redcurrants, raspberries, strawberries. My dad's *pièce de résistance* was his amazing chrysanthemums, which were coveted from Heeley to Parson's Cross, and these too we were able to sell to supplement the budget and the savings for the summer holiday.

Although Mum and Dad often took me with them to the allotment on summer evenings, they never managed to interest me in gardening, and I remain a clueless gardener to this day. Nevertheless, if I did not inherit my father's horticultural skills, which oddly enough have skipped a generation and seem to be in my children's blood, on the other hand I did inherit his love of sport. From May through to September, he played cricket on Saturday afternoons and often in a midweek league also. He was an all-rounder, an excellent fielder, and a sound batsman, but his strength was his bowling. He bowled medium pace seamers on a nagging length that frustrated and bamboozled opponents. Most of all, he just loved playing. I never saw him play football, at least I don't remember seeing him. He had certainly given up playing by the time I started school, when he would have been touching forty.

Dad, after scoring 57, his pal Bill Jakeman behind

Dad had very little schooling, but he was an avid bedtime reader. Of cowboy books, which Mum borrowed from the Lowfields library for him. The Heeley Green Picture House was a great source of cowboy films. Buck Jones, Hopalong Cassidy, Gene Autry and Roy Rogers were the principal names I remember from that time. It seems to me now that our nights out, Dad and I, to see a cowboy film at the Heeley Green happened almost every Wednesday night. We would rush off after tea to catch the 'first house', which started sometime after six. If we missed the minor feature, a cartoon or the Pathetone news, we could always stay on for the 'second house' to see it, unless Dad decided it was bedtime. Amongst us Heeley lads, you were either a Gene Autry man or a Roy Rogers man, and I was in the Gene Autry camp. I don't know about Dad. I found Gene Autry casual, but tough - in today's terms, a really cool guy. Roy Rogers did too much singing for my liking, and I took a dislike to his albino eyelashes and his fancy outfits. Nor was I too keen on his pristine white horse, Trigger, which was all too fond of dressage tricks. Sorry, Roy, nothing personal. I was also fond of good old Gabby Hayes, who was sometimes called Windy Halliday in films. Gabby appeared perpetually on the brink of a nervous breakdown, but he was light relief from the drama, had an entertaining voice, and was often a source of crucial information for the 'good guys'. I don't remember Dad ever expressing whether or not he had enjoyed these films, but he kept on taking me to see them week after week, and so I can safely assume that he did.

In my case, close rivals for favourite film genre were the Robin Hood and the Tarzan films. My pal Ray Smith and I loved trying to emulate the ape man in Cat Lane Woods. We were quite good at the ape calls, but our efforts at swinging through the trees were mostly limited to hanging from a low bough. I have a few hazy impressions of the many Tarzan films that I saw – Johnny Weissmuller swinging effortlessly from vine to vine through tree after tree, yodelling; Maureen O'Sullivan as Jane, looking beautiful and tidying up their treetop home. Both sported immaculately tailored loincloths, Weissmuller all sculpted musculature, luxuriant locks and perfectly clean shaven, O'Hara the image of feminine beauty with not a hair out of place.

Cheeta, their chimpanzee friend, was an ever-present in the films we saw. His function was to add an element of humour, as well as to provide Tarzan and Jane with a warning signal that evil was close by. Later on, to our delight, the couple acquired a son, played by the actor Johnny Sheffield, whose name brought the jungle family even closer to our hearts. As to the stories, there was always a danger, in the form of crocodiles, which allowed Tarzan to show off his Olympian[6] swimming prowess, perilous treks through the jungle, evil white men up to no good, exploiting the jungle and the animal kingdom, often out to kill elephants for their tusks, encounters with snakes, swamps and quicksands, which swallowed down the unwary, who then had to be rescued heroically by Tarzan.

My favourite positive memory of all the Tarzan films was the scene in which the secret elephant graveyard, fervently sought by the evil white men, is revealed in all its stark and

---

[6] *Among Weissmuller's legendary swimming triumphs were five Olympic gold medals and 67 world records.*

solemn grandeur. On the other hand, the mere thought of slipping into a swamp or a quicksand still sends a cold frisson down my spine. Nevertheless, thanks to Tarzan, I do know how to deal with quicksand crises, and so, if the emergency ever arises, I'm your man. Just call me on my mobile. My Tarzan skills do not, however, extend to dealing with snakes, and even though I am familiar with the forked stick technique, my snake-work leaves quite a lot to be desired.

My pal Ray Smith and I continued to be aficionados of the Tarzan films well into our high teens. Dad liked them too, I think.

As to Robin Hood, I loved those romps in Sherwood Forest, those tales of Good versus Evil, where I was always confident that the hero would triumph in the end. It was disappointing that Robin was played by a different actor every time, which seemed to call for a disturbing switch of loyalties. My favourite Robin was without doubt Richard Todd, in the 1952 version[7], closely rivalled by Erroll Flynn in an older, pre-war film. Anyone who has seen both interpretations will understand my confusion about Robin's true personality. The moment I loved best in these adventures – and I have no idea which film it was – is when King Richard returns from the Crusades, recovers his rightful throne from the usurper Prince John and dubs Robin a knight in reward for his loyalty to the true king. I used to imagine myself kneeling before the king one distant day and hearing the words 'Arise, Sir John of Heeley'. So far, there has been not even so much as an MBE, but I remain optimistic.

Later on, in my early teens, the short feature before the main film became *Captain Marvel*, and this was soon another obsession of mine. The cunning ploy of cinemas at the time was that two of these episodes were shown per week, Monday to Wednesday for the first episode, then Thursday to Saturday for the next, ensuring that fans of Captain Marvel had to make twice-weekly visits to the Heeley Green, so

---

[7] *A glance at the cast list reveals a long list of star names that you will recognise, including Peter Finch, James Hayter, James Robertson Justice, Michael Hordern, Patrick Barr, Bill Owen, and Hubert Gregg.*

as not to lose the thread of the story. These were not animations, by the way, but real actors. When Captain Marvel or Mary Marvel flew, they were shown hanging by a wire, floating lifelessly across a backdrop of artificial sky. Even we children were aware that the images were totally unrealistic, but we suspended our disbelief willingly. The acting was lousy, the stories were naff, but we loved it all and spoke of little else in Heeley. The word 'shazam!' was rarely far from our lips.

Going to t' pictures, or t' flicks, played a major role in family life of the post-war years, especially during the dark evenings. As well as a good selection in the city centre, we were well blessed locally with picture houses. In addition to the Heeley Green, at the bottom of Gleadless Road was the Heeley Palace, and, a short walk from there, the Heeley Coliseum. My memory of the Heeley Palace was that it was slightly classier than the Heeley Green, whereas the Heeley Coliseum was regarded as more downmarket. However, it was at the Coliseum that I saw my first ever film, *Pinocchio*, one afternoon with Mum and Auntie Annie. Whilst I remember this as an intriguing, entertaining and amusing experience, a window into a new world of wonders, which kept me from my afternoon nap, I also learned that there were bad things happening in the world when your mum is not there to look after you, and I was in no hurry to repeat the experience. I have been told that I was also taken to see *Bambi* and wept bitterly throughout, but I have wiped all traces of this trauma from my memory.

Saturday evenings were usually reserved for the Abbeydale Picture House, which showed more up-to-date films. It wasn't possible to reserve seats in advance, and Saturday night was a favourite time for picture-goers. For popular films, this resulted in a queue snaking all along the front side of the cinema and down Bedale Road. If your position in the queue was halfway down Bedale Road, then it was touch and go whether you would get in to see the 'big picture', and at the very least you were likely to miss the first part of the evening's entertainment, the cartoon and Pathetone News. One big bonus for us youngsters going to the Abbeydale was the tiny drinks shop alongside the picture-house. It was an odd little shop which sold odd little things, like health foods, vitamins, root beer and, most importantly, sarsaparilla, which in their usual, idiosyncratic way everybody in Sheffield called 'sasparella'. I am not at all sure what was the attraction of 'sasparella'; it was black, flat, sickly sweet with hints of liquorice, and frankly tasted pretty dire. Yet we clamoured for it, and adults seemed to think it was good for us.

Saturday nights were usually the time for comedy films, starring Tommy Trinder, George Formby, Alistair Sim, Alec Guinness, Abbot and Costello, Old Mother Riley (and Kitty MacShane, of course), and many others. My Uncle Tom was that man whose great roar of laughter can be heard throughout the auditorium. You always knew when he was present in the audience on a Saturday night. He loved Frank Randall and Bob Hope beyond measure, and I was infected by his enthusiasm and loved them too. Hearing him laugh somewhere in the picture house always reassured me that all was well with the world. If Uncle Tom was happy, then I was happier still. I never met anyone fuller of *joie de vivre* than my uncle Tom. With him amongst the company, there was bound to be hilarity and raucous good humour. Thomas Billard had served from 1942 to 1946 in Burma and had many stories ranging from hilarious to gruesome, though not one of them about the war, which he never mentioned. To hear him, you might have believed he had been on an extended jungle jolly. I am sure he had not. One other thing about Tom: he never let a drop of alcohol pass his lips. Another matter he never spoke about. He gave me his field hat, which I considered the essence of style. He also gave me my first cigarette. One Christmas Day, when my cousin David and I were 15 and 14 respectively, he took us aside and shoved a packet of Woodbines into my hand: 'You don't want to be with these old folk, so get off out and smoke a cig or two.' Actually, I did want to be with these old folk, but we went off obediently, walked up Gleadless Road, smoked a few, coughed a lot, and felt sick. Then we came home to enjoy the party games.

Uncle Tom Billard

Unlike Uncle Tom, Dad was a man of few words, never using two when one would do. Nor was he extravagant in issuing praise or blame. His highest level of praise was to say that something was 'reight enough'. He was a quiet man, even at football matches, although I do remember a row with a man standing behind us who was swearing too much for Dad's liking. Too many 'chuffings' and 'bleedings', I think[8], although I can't say that I had noticed, as I was far

---

[8] *A comment on attitudes to swearing: The euphemism 'flipping' was not considered swearing, and 'flippin eely' (flipping Heeley) was the most common curse among us youngsters. 'Bloody' and 'bugger' were common enough, but would have been disapproved of in mixed company, while 'chuffing', 'sod' and 'sodding' were regarded as coarse, 'bleeding' was considered worse still, and 'blinding' absolutely beyond the pale. The F word I never heard until I went to University, and then only from the cockier students, the C word even later still. I was 20 before I heard a man use the F-word in the street in the company of women, and I was shocked.*

too absorbed in the football. Dad was a keen follower of the Blades and rarely missed a home match at Bramall Lane. Mum and I went with him from as early as I can remember, in 1946, I suppose, I a tiny boy who had to stand on Dad's toolbox to watch. I clasped it under my arm down Richards Road and over Havelock Bridge, aware even at that tender age of that electricity in the air before a big event, the signal that it was the weekend and people were free. I have no idea how the adults felt after six long years of war, but it must have been a special feeling.

There were few women at the match, and so my mum stood out somewhat amongst the thousands of identikit flat-capped men, but I never felt that this was strange. Like the cinema, the football match was something the working class could afford, at one shilling per adult and sixpence per child, behind the goal. The working class did not stand at the side of the ground or sit in the stands, as this was too expensive. Bramall Lane was a bit of an exception, as one side of the pitch had no spectators, being separated from the action by the county cricket pitch and therefore too far away for a good view. We always stood in exactly the same spot, at the front of the top section of the Spion Kop[9], above a footway and so well elevated above the crowd below.

The greatly anticipated event of the football season was always the Christmas match, either on Boxing Day at 3 pm, or Christmas Day at 11 am. The Sheffield teams always had a fixture on both days, against the same opponents, home and away, an arrangement repeated on Easter Saturday and Easter Monday. The Christmas Day home match was a much-loved ritual, with all the menfolk attending, including Uncle Harry and my cousin Peter, who lived in Maltby. Everyone was happy and imbued with the seasonal spirit, and, already high on the euphoria of the bounty left by Father Christmas, I flew down the hill to Bramall Lane full of expectation. Even if we lost, the uphill trudge back home was not so bad, as the festive dinner with all Mum's family was

---

[9] *The Spion Kop was mostly called t' Shoreham Street End. It was never called just The Kop (or more correctly T' Kop) for short in those days. I would guess this abbreviation is an infection contracted later from Liverpudlians.*

next, to be followed by an evening of party games and high spirits. These times were when my dad came out of his shell and became his true self, laughing, teasing Auntie Annie mercilessly, making jokes, pulling Grandma's leg.

I was an avid reader of the *Green Un*, the Star's Saturday sport edition on green paper. From half past five, a long straggling line of men, and boys like me, addicts all, would queue outside the newsagents, on tenterhooks, waiting for the arrival of the *Star* van with their Saturday hit of football news. The driver would screech to a halt, fling a bundle of *Green Uns*, tied up with rough string, onto the pavement and roar away again, on to the next newsagent. The *Green Un* must get through! I would devour the paper, consume every report, every detail. I especially loved the cartoons by Harry Heap, which reported in a witty and whimsical style on the afternoon's proceedings at Bramall Lane or Hillsborough, in five or six captioned drawings, usually ending with a sardonic comment by Alf, an old cynic in a flat cap and striped scarf. Matches finished at twenty to five at the earliest, and the whole paper was completed to a five o'clock deadline. The *Green Un*, its van drivers, printers, reporters, editors and especially Harry Heap were a wonder of press efficiency. And all this without computers, software or even mobile phones.

I was a true addict for football statistics. I had an eidetic memory where sport was concerned. I knew the name of every football ground, the colour of the club shirts and shorts, the clubs with the highest attendances, the team's nickname, and after an hour with the *Green Un*, scouring the results, the half-time scores and the standings in the Football League and the Scottish League, on the lookout for victories by underdogs, recoveries from impossible half-time situations, high scores and high aggregate scores, I was able to tell you how any team had fared on that day. I was the Leslie Welch[10] of the *Green Un*.

As football has always played such a leading role in my life-story, a few words about my own chequered allegiances

---

[10] *Leslie Welch (1907-1980) was a stage and radio entertainer who was nicknamed the Memory Man. He was later in television and films.*

seem appropriate at this point. We have established that I lived near Bramall Lane, and that my parents followed United, and so it was inevitable that I follow United. Yes, as night is destined to follow day, I was destined to follow the Blades. It was in my stars, in my genes, and in my postal district, Sheffield 2.[11]

Until I was seven. Or was it eleven?

One June day in 1947, I read in the *Green Un* that Sheffield Wednesday had led 2-1 at Saltergate, the home ground of the mighty Chesterfield FC,[12] before conceding no fewer than three penalties to lose 2-4. I had been keeping a close eye on the fortunes of United's suffering neighbours in Division 2 and already felt sorry for them, as they had been in constant danger of a degrading relegation to Division 3, whereas the Blades were lording it at the top end of Division 1. This business of the penalties was the last straw. What dreadfully bad luck! My heart went out to them. The following season I started to sneak away on the tram from Heeley Bottom to watch Wednesday on the alternate Saturdays when they were at home. I fell for the blue and white stripes and the Brylcreem. I stood at the railings directly behind the Penistone Road end goal. It was a different feeling from Bramall Lane. Make no mistake, I liked the Blades, I admired the Blades, but this was special, this appealed directly to the soul. I felt the roar of the crowd in my gut, like an animal inside me.

I continued to watch both teams and wanted both to win, but the day came, on September 8th, 1951, when the two teams clashed at Bramall Lane. United prevailed, by 7 goals to 3, and I was devastated. Dad found me clinging to the railings behind the goal, weeping scalding tears, long after most had gone home. I knew then where my heart lay. This humiliation would not be forgotten, nor forgiven. I was no longer a Unitedite.

---

[11] *In 1995 I returned to Sheffield 2, and still live there.*

[12] *For the uninitiated, Chesterfield FC is anything but mighty. This is irony.*

Heap's cartoon, Jan 5, 1952. 65,384 saw Owls 1-3 Blades, same season as the 7-3. Owls were to be champions that season, with 100 goals, Blades finished 11th

The weekly highlights of my Annexe years, which fed my ravenous hunger both for reading and for sport and adventure, arrived like clockwork on Tuesdays and Thursdays of every week of the year, in the form of *Wizard, Adventure, Hotspur* and *Rover*[13], two of them on Tuesdays, two on Thursdays. They were not in the comic strip form of later years, but regular magazines of pure text, with probably one title picture per story. Each magazine contained six episodes of the series of tales published for that season, and as boys' magazines go, they were pretty well written. Mum ordered them from Woolhouses' newsagents and they cost twopence each. I was a spoilt child! Mum and Dad probably judged that reading was just the ticket for me. And it was. What a godsend for a sport-mad lad like me to have such a cornucopia of tales provided week after week after week, in seem-

---

[13] *All published by the DC Thomson Group*

ingly endless variety, from the ages of eight to twelve! I would love even now to relive the thrill of picking up the brand new, uncreased copies, full of the promise of new episodes about my own personal heroes. Personal heroes, because I didn't know anyone else who read them.

I loved the sport stories, of course. There were plenty of football heroes to admire. Limp Along Lesley lived as a shepherd on the North Yorkshire Moors and had a crippled leg, which gave him the power to curve the ball in unexpected directions and win many a lost cause by bamboozling the opposition. Baldy Hogan, well into his forties and therefore old in my eyes, was player-coach of a mediocre league team and won many a match by his cunning tactics and superior ball skills. Another character I recall was Billy "Cannonball" Kidd, a schoolboy whose goal-scoring feats ensured success for a team of veterans returning from war, and I have a vague memory of "the goalie with magnetic hands". The *It's the . . . That Count* series, which changed sport and title with the season of the year, began with Nick Smith and *It's goals that count*, but in the summer it was Rob Higdon and *It's Runs That Count,* which morphed into *It's Fielding That Counts* and *It's Wickets That Count* in subsequent years. There were always cheats and malevolent characters out to thwart our heroes in every episode, but right always triumphed in the end, even if it took the whole series.

It was in the athletics stories where I met the two true superheroes of the forties and early fifties, Alf Tupper, The Tough of the Track, and Wilson, the great Corinthian. Athletes were amateurs, and so Wilson never won more than a medal, and Alf may have won the odd canteen of cutlery. The two were poles apart as characters. Alf was a hundred percent realistic to me. He was a rough lad, pugnacious, a rebel, and totally working class. He earned a pittance as a welder and, at the time I knew him, worked and slept in Smith's Yard, under railway arches, in the grim northern town of Greystone. Like Dad and me, he had bread and dripping for breakfast, when he could get it, and otherwise I don't recall him ever eating anything else but fish and chips, straight from the newspaper. Unlike Wilson, he was occasionally beaten into second place, although he always learned from defeat. He hated the athletics establishment who were always out to thwart him. He also frequently had to rescue someone from deadly peril, before or even during a race.

The one Alf Tupper story that sticks out in my memory – and even I thought that it took some swallowing – was when Alf worked on Saturday morning, was poisoned by carbon monoxide, fell into a coma, was discovered by Smith, was shaken back to his senses, and found there was only half an hour to the start of an important race. He sprang up, donned his spikes, vest and shorts, ran several miles to the track, with a deathly headache, buying and eating fish and chips on the run, arrived at the starting line as the runners lined up, broke the four-minute mile and fell back into the coma.

Wilson, in complete contrast, was unreal. For a start, he was over a hundred and fifty years old, went permanently bare-footed, and wore at all times a Victorian-style athletics outfit, a black one-piece leotard of sorts. He was triumphant at any athletics event he took on. The first time he appeared in print, this admittedly well before my years of reading the tales, he had run a mile event in three minutes flat, immediately falling into a coma afterwards. He could leap over seven feet high and 28 feet long[14], as well as hurling the shot, discus, javelin and hammer phenomenal distances. He lived on the wild Moors of the North of England and Scotland, living on a secret diet of herbs, nuts and berries. I believe he was not above chasing down a rabbit or a deer and eating it.

The two Wilson stories that I remember best, however, did not involve athletics. One was a challenge match on a deserted island against a football team owned by an evil Russian millionaire. The Russian's team, who played in all black, was made up of eleven players so physically strong and fit that he claimed them to be unbeatable. Wilson took ten ordinary lads, trained them and coached them so brilliantly that they were able to travel to the island to vanquish the evil black automata. I do not recall how the clash of col-

---

[14] *Both these records were, ironically to be beaten by mere real humans.*

ours between the black team and Wilson's leotard was resolved.

The second story was when the England cricket team did not arrive in time for the first Ashes test. Were they all killed in a plane crash? Kidnapped? Whatever. At all events, Wilson had to put together a team of ex-pats to win the Ashes in Australia. He chose tubby, middle-aged chaps, explaining that, because they couldn't bend down, they would be excellent at stopping the ball with their feet. The match was over before tea. Wilson bowled at 120 mph from one end and skittled the Aussies out in three overs. The balls which missed the stumps smashed the sightscreen into smithereens. A few runs were conceded from the other end and quite a few byes from Wilson's end, but the selection of the arthritic fielders was justified by their brilliant footwork.

Wilson hammered the ball around the ground when it was England's turn to bat, whilst his team-mates were all out for a duck. He scored enough for England to win by an innings, after he had skittled the Aussies a second time.

In the strange world of the DC Thomson boys' magazines, there were no women. None of my heroes had a girlfriend, let alone a wife. At least none was ever mentioned. Mothers were either invisible or deceased. All my heroes were loners, outsiders, many of them let down by the world. Alf Tupper and Limp Along Lesley were both orphans and solitary figures, as was Wilson, who was entirely detached from the real world. Perhaps this was their appeal for many a young lad who loved these stories.

Last but not least, there were the stories of Red Circle School, an English Public School and a boarding school. I became engrossed in these stories, in the adventures of the boys of the Lower Fourth, the Remove, or the Sixth Form, of Mr Smugg, the vindictive housemaster of Home House, of bullies and cheats, of kind and just Cripple Dick Archer the prefect, stories of dorms, of prep, of being gated, of sixth formers making toast in their study. I longed to be part of it, wanted to play in the House matches, to sleep with the other chaps in a dorm. It tasted of freedom and adventure.

Sometime in 1952, there was a competition to win one of fifty leather footballs, 'caseys'. All you had to do to win was cut out all the photos of footballers in all the editions of *Adventure, Wizard, Hotspur* and *Rover* for four consecutive weeks and send them to the publisher with your entry form. I hated cutting out the pictures because it spoiled the magazine and removed important chunks from the stories. The consolation was that I knew I had won, as I had collected all the pictures and could not be beaten. I waited for the results to be published, barely sleeping at night for excitement. When they appeared, my name was not among the winners, who were youth clubs, schools and scout troupes, who had amalgamated their pictures and sent in hundreds. I felt cheated and fell into a depression. A few weeks later I began to notice that the same stories that I had read years previously were appearing again, word for word. I had put my faith and trust in my friends at *Adventure, Rover, Hotspur* and *Wizard*, and they had betrayed me with false promises. I asked Mum to cancel my subscription. After all, I still had Biggles, Algy and Ginger, and William Brown and the Outlaws.

III   Early days

I have a few memories of the war years, but whether they are true or imagined, my own or merely stories I was told, I am unable to say, and these memories come with that caveat. Of my paternal grandmother I have no recollection whatsoever, as she died before I was born, but I remember my grandad, Ernest William Foster, as the little man who came every washday and sat on a dining chair just inside the back door saying, as far as I can remember, nothing. He died towards the end of the war, but sadly I remember no sense of loss, of missing him, no period of mourning, nor even a sense that he was no longer present on washdays. I know only that whenever I was naughty or mischievous, my mum used to say, affectionately I think, that it was the Ernest William coming out in me.

While we're on the subject of naughty or mischievous, I recall a strange custom that I developed in my early years, although I hasten to add that I have grown out of it now. Whenever I was 'showing off' or generally behaving like a spoilt brat, my parents would send me upstairs to my room. I, however, worked out a cunning plan. By now I had learned to unlock and unbolt the front door, and so I crept silently and stealthily back downstairs and made my escape through the front door onto Northcote Road. From there I would walk 'round the lump' (about 300 yards) and come back into the house through the back door, where I would behave as if nothing had happened. My parents were probably surprised the first time I did this and, either on purpose or out of pure shock,

Dad on left, Grandfather Ernest William on right (sister Louisa's wedding)

kept a straight face and played along with my cunning plan. It suited me just fine, and as it turns out, it seemed to suit them too. Honour was upheld, face was saved, and the slate was wiped clean. On reflection, it really was quite a cunning plan. Perhaps I should have followed a diplomatic career.

There are two pals from my pre-school days who merit an honourable mention in this memoir, Pat Lee and Stanley Platts, if only for the affection which they clearly stirred in me as a small child. Pat was my age and lived in the last house at the top of the lane. We were inseparable for a while and I was constantly asking if Pat could come for tea. She did come a couple of times. We were playing out in the lane together on one occasion when I was called in for my bath. I asked if Pat could come and play in the bath with me, a perfectly reasonable request, and had a bit of a paddy when this boon was not granted. Mum seemed to think it was all very amusing.

Stanley was at least five years older than I, probably more, but I regarded him as a pal and treated him as an equal. I was likewise forever asking Mum if Stanley could come for tea, or if he could come with us on an outing. This became something of a family joke, although I meant it in earnest. He must have been a very tolerant lad, especially when I would knock on his door and ask 'Can your Stanley come out to play, Mrs Platts?'

Pat disappeared out of my life sometime during primary school years, I know not whither, and Stanley no doubt went off and did things boys five or seven years older did. There is still a tiny hole in my life where they both used to be.

As for the war, I know we had an Anderson shelter in the back garden, because I played in there often after the war, until it was removed in about 1948. It was an excellent den, except in wet weather when the interior turned into one muddy puddle. This corrugated iron air raid shelter was sunk two or three feet into the garden, had a curved roof and was covered with the earth that had been dug up. It formed a great mound at the bottom of the garden, where I could stand and be king of the castle. It had three steps leading down into it and seats on either side for three or four people. I remember it as having no door, but it obviously would have had one originally. I don't remember us ever taking shelter there, as our house was the one in the yard which had a reinforced ceiling in the cellar. There was also a little door, barely two foot square, low down in the brick wall between our cellar and the neighbouring cellar, through which the Kendall family had to climb, along with their camp-stools, when the siren sounded in the night to announce a threatened air raid. Poor old Mrs Woodhouse, who lived in the corner house and whose body shape was approximately one yard cubed, had to squeeze through two of these tiny trapdoors to reach safety. By the time she had reached the second escape door she was on the point of collapse, and my father and Tom Kendall had to drag her through unceremoniously and with embarrassing exposure of bloomers into the haven of number 16, as she gasped over and over 'Missis, your lass', a phrase I remember her using whenever she was flustered or felt things were getting out of hand.

One memorable event towards the end of the war was the day we received the food parcel, from Canada. It was very heavy and arrived plastered with all kinds of labels and official stamps. My mum and dad, Grandma, and Auntie Annie and Uncle Ron gathered round it for the official opening.

The contents, though interesting, were less exciting than I had hoped. There were four bars of what was called chocolate, but which turned out to be waxy and tasteless and smelled a bit mouldy. There were a few tins of corned beef of Argentine origin and some of spam, as well as two tins of peaches in syrup, which I liked, and a large tin of marrowfat peas, which I didn't. There was also a large package of something called 'locusts', a sort of hard, seedy, dried fruit, the dark colour of a very old banana[15], difficult to chew and disgusting to eat. Life could be disappointing at times.

I remember with great clarity my mum informing me that the war was over and me dashing round to my grandma's house in the next yard to tell her the wonderful news. I think that was probably VE Day, but it may well have been VJ Day. I shall never know. I do remember the huge bonfire in the lane between our yard and Mrs Morley's and Mrs Shaw's on the opposite side, and I remember being very happy that all the grown-ups were so happy and hugging and kissing people they didn't normally hug and kiss. Even at this tender age I was aware of the name Churchill, which was on everyone's lips and seemed to provoke a degree of universal admiration. Equally, I was aware that my mum did not like Churchill, because of the face she pulled when his name was mentioned. When I was older it became very clear that she hated the man and regarded him as a bully and an enemy of the working class and trade unions. She also told me about the atrocities that he had committed in India as a younger man, how he was a racist and white supremacist, considering the white man as a 'higher grade race', a man who had no compunction about using poison gas against primitive peoples. She had not forgotten his responsibility for the murderous Dardanelles expedition of World War I. My mother was a kind and loving woman, but it became very clear to me that she hated Churchill and continued to do so all her life. She had her own special portmanteau word for the way he spoke and his general atti-

---

[15] *I should mention here that at the time I had no idea what a very old banana looked like, as I had never yet seen a banana, new or old.*

tude, 'sleering', which I took to be a combination of sneering, slurring, and slimy.

The contempt for Churchill ran along with a very clear message that I learned early in my life, that Conservatives were bad and Labour was good. Mum was a member of the local Labour Party, friends with several local councillors and a strong supporter of the Cooperative movement and the Cooperative Women's Guild. She would have made an excellent and conscientious councillor herself, but was far too modest to aspire to such heights. One more thing about Mum, which is in its own way the measure of the woman: she was a regular blood donor from 1942 until her mastectomy in 1962, when she was obliged to give up giving. Her collection of certificates and her long service badge are safe with me for the moment. Bless you, Mum.

The new Heeley parliamentary constituency was a different animal from the Heeley I lived in. It replaced the staunchly Conservative Ecclesall ward. I remember the 1950 General Election clearly enough, from my own 10-year-old perspective, of course. I remember all the red posters declaring 'Vote Jennings!' with a regrettably unimpressive looking picture of Mr Jennings on them. I remember walking along with some pals, singing 'Vote, vote, vote for Mr Jennings! You can't vote for a better man!' I remember the freezing cold fingertips I got from shoving hundreds of leaflets through letter-boxes with my mum. I was sure Jennings would win. How could he lose, in Heeley? Surely the last election result had been a mistake. Labour clung onto office by the skin of their teeth, and Arnold Jennings was soundly defeated by the incumbent Tory member, Sir Peter Roberts, 3rd baronet. Perhaps it was a valuable early political education. Nevertheless, I have consistently found Mum's theory, 'Labour good, Conservative bad', to hold water. Now as then, Labour has always held the moral high ground.

The post-war period must have been a happier, more relaxed time, but I can't say that I noticed much difference. I remember some treats, for instance the arrival on the scene of the 'Joystick', which could only be obtained at the post office and cost twopence, twice as much as Mrs Memmott's flookyops. The Joystick was a Toblerone-shaped ice lolly in a cardboard case, five or six inches long. You tore open the top end of the cardboard to reveal the lolly and then pushed it up gradually with your thumb, as you sucked it away, bit by bit. It was a wonderful new ritual!

Shortly after that, I was introduced to the orange. I tried a couple of segments, but they were a bit sour for my liking. At some stage after that came a new yellow and brown fruit called a banana, but I have to confess that I found it underwhelming also. I by far preferred joysticks and flookypops. Some kind friend of Grandma's sent me some pieces of coconut to try. It may have been tainted, as I have had an almost allergic dislike to coconut ever since, particularly the desiccated kind.

I was soon aware of the phenomenon of The Great National Sporting Event. Two great national sporting events, the Epsom Derby and the FA Cup Final, were the first to make their mark on me. We all listened enthralled to both, gathered around grandma's wireless round at number 10.

The Cup Final was an all-day affair which seemed to get everyone very excited, even my grandma, who knew nothing about football. I was on the edge of my stool the whole afternoon. I knew some of the players, as I had acquired a few cigarette cards, with pictures of Sam Bartram, the Charlton Athletic goalie, Peter Doherty and Raich Carter, both Derby County players, who were reputed to be brilliant. The match went to extra time, and then Derby County ran out 4-1 winners. I felt sorry for Charlton Athletic and very glad when they were allowed to win the following year, as a sort of consolation, which seemed fair to me.

As to the Derby, I liked the name Airborne and chose it as my horse. I was disappointed to find that according to my Uncle Harry, Airborne had no chance of winning, because it only had three legs. Surprisingly, it did win, despite its tripedal handicap, to the delight of my mum, who told me I was very clever. Fortunately, I was too young to let this early success go to my head.

I find it a great sadness that we remember so little of our infancy, for most of us the happiest, most serene days of our life, secure in the knowledge that whatever happens Mum and Dad, grandparents, aunts and uncles will be there to keep us safe, to feed us, to shelter us, to love us. I suppose I must be content with the knowledge that these carefree early years build a strong foundation for our development as children, adolescents and adults. I speak for myself and my own extended family here, but it would be callous of me to ignore the fact that so many millions of children are not so lucky and experience wretched childhoods. For them, erasing memories of infancy is often a blessing rather than a curse. My heart goes out to them. I was one of the lucky ones.

IV 16 Northcote Road: at home with Mum

I was born into a comparatively poor family, but poverty features in no way in any of the memories of my years in Heeley. I don't remember ever going hungry, only that food and clothing, treats and outings were basic and simple. Most of my friends were from similarly hard-pressed families, and what you don't have you don't miss. Pleasures and pastimes cost little or nothing then – marbles, fivestones, hopscotch, football and cricket in the street or the park, cowboys and Indians. We were free to roam the streets and the woods, we cooperated, we negotiated, we organised ourselves, we learned to distinguish fair from unfair, kind from cruel, teamwork from competition, loyalty and friendship from fickleness. We came home covered in muck, knees scuffed and scabbed, hands and face grimy. We were happy enough, we had fun, and like all kids we were sometimes bored.

Northcote Road began as a wide cobbled street with its unbroken terrace of houses for 120 yards or so along a flat area, and then narrowed and sloped steeply down a long line of more modern semi-detached houses, built in the 1930s and owner occupied. Posh houses to us. Even into my teenage years, there were no cars parked on our section of Northcote Road. If we ever saw a car, it meant that someone was poorly enough for the doctor to visit. The dividing line was made painfully obvious by the change in gradient and the invisibility of the posh houses from where I lived. Number 16 was part of this line of about 25 houses stretching along the top part of Northcote Road, all attached one to the next but divided into 'yards' of three houses. All but the first two yards, ours and my grandma's, were accessible from the front via a passage.

As a little boy, I always regarded myself as living in Carrfield[16] Lane, but I knew that my real address was 16 Northcote Road. Carrfield Lane was a cobbled alleyway some six or seven yards across with a central gutter. It served the rear entrances to houses on Carrfield Road and the first few houses in Northcote Road. When asked where I lived, I would answer 'I live down the Lane', unless I was asked specifically for my address. The lane ran the length of the top section of my street and terminated at iron railings and two narrow gennels leading to Northcote Road and Carrfield Road. I went to check recently and found that a quarter of the lane is still there, but it is now blocked off by a brick wall just before the spot where our house stood.

Our front door was rarely used, except for visits from the doctor, or on the rare occasion it had to be opened to pay the coalman, or to receive a parcel from the postman. Otherwise, it remained locked and bolted for most of the year. Routine visitors, like the milkman or the rent-collector, always came to the back door. Almost opposite our front door was the church hall of Heeley St Peter's Mission Church, which was to play a central part in the leisure activities and social life of my childhood and teen years. As I recall, it was Hobson's choice, as there was nowhere else to socialise indoors!

The house was small, a so-called two-up two-down terrace. The doors opened directly onto the back yard and a postage stamp front garden with a low wall and iron railings, the latter soon to be sacrificed for the war effort. We had two downstairs rooms, both ten-foot square with linoleum floor covering, the kitchen at the back and 'the room' at the front, with a bay window. The kitchen served also as living-room, dining-room and bathroom. The lavatory was about 20 yards away at the bottom of the back yard, and

---

[16] Several street names in the Heeley/Meersbrook area of Sheffield include Carrfield or its variant Carfield, as in Carfield School, my own school.

the cistern tended to freeze up on winter nights, which obliged us to install a small paraffin lamp. As toilet paper we used cut-up squares of the Sheffield Star, impaled on a nail. In the kitchen-cum-living room was a fireplace for coal fires and a small range, used for baking and cooking. Mum took great pride in keeping a gleaming range and fire-grate, which she maintained by sheer elbow grease and regular black-leading. First, she cleaned out the ashes and scrubbed the grate, sometimes with meths, then she applied the black lead, a commercially produced paste, to the grate and the range and buffed it up with a shoe brush and a polishing cloth.

On the hearth, as in every house, were the coal scuttle, a set of fire irons, comprising a poker, a pair of tongs for arranging the hot coals, a brush and shovel and the indispensable toasting-fork. Being allowed to toast your own bread on the fire for the first time was an early rite of passage! The mantelpiece, which we called the 'cornish' always carried a pair of wooden candlesticks, several ornaments, a tea-caddy, a packet of my dad's *Park Drive*, and my money box[17].

Hanging from a hook at the right-hand end of the mantelpiece was the strop, sometimes called the strap. The strop, a flexible leather belt, was ostensibly for sharpening cutthroat razors, but in working class homes also hung as the symbol of paternal authority, or more generally male authority. As I have no memory of my dad
ever using anything other than a Wardonia safety
razor[18] and blades, then symbolic it must have been. I know that most children feared the threat "I'll get the strap down to you if you don't behave", and I was aware of a certain baleful aura surrounding it just hanging there. Dad never

---

[17] *For the sake of historical accuracy, I should add that this money box was the head and shoulders of a black African boy, who took your coin in his hand and swallowed it. Many children had one of these money boxes. We called it 'the nigger'. I wince as I write the offensive word. As a child, I was blissfully unaware of the implicit racism.*

[18] *Mum did later confide to me, most disloyally I thought, that once in his younger days Dad had taken up the cut-throat razor, but had ended up looking like a half-hearted suicide.*

took his strop down to me, nor even threatened to, but even though I could hardly have been regarded as a difficult child, the silent but visible menace of the strop remained a constant presence.

An afterthought. A very recent and disagreeable experience reminded me how attitudes betrayed by the strop cling on to this day:

Out walking on Easter Sunday, 2021, a pristine afternoon, with new life everywhere, I see a young couple coming towards me, both scarcely into their twenties. The man strides ahead with his dog, the woman behind with a pushchair, in it a sobbing baby, under two. The man turns and points at child aggressively: "Shut it!" The child does not shut it. The man leans over child, raises his hand, threatening to strike a blow: "Do you want another?" The child falls silent. The man turns to his dog and ruffles the fur on its neck affectionately: "Come on, lad."

I wonder what lesson has been learned here? I want to speak, but they and the moment are past. And he is angry and six decades younger and stronger.

To the left of the chimney breast were the enamel draining board and sink, which served as both kitchen and bathroom sink. There was only a single cold-water tap until sometime in the early 1950s, when a gas geezer was installed above the sink. Beside the sink there was an electric 'copper' to heat water for washday and bath-night. Washday Mondays meant that the house smelled damp and was full of steam. It also meant that Mum had to haul the heavy washday equipment up from the cellar: the zinc washtub and bucket, the wringer, or mangle, and the ridged wooden washboard. She filled the copper using a hosepipe from the kitchen tap, plugged in, switched on and waited till the water boiled. I still have the copper posser she used to beat and stir the laundry in the zinc tub. I have never had the heart to throw it out. I have no first-hand experience of washing a week's laundry by hand, but the process required a lot of exertion and must have been exhausting as well as complicated, with all the various stages, the washing, the scrubbing, the rinsing, the wringing, the filling up and the emptying out of the tub. There may have often been bleaching too, although Dad's work hardly required starched collars, and so this was one chore that Mum was largely spared at least. She did, however, have to starch the collars and cuffs[19] of his 'best' shirts. There was also the crucial introduction of a little blue bag, or blue dolly, at some stage, which I understand was to ensure the whites became whiter than white, a theory that has never made complete sense to me. Then there was the tiresome pegging-out-on-the-line and then fetching-back-in-and-folding business. I have often helped with the tedious stretching and folding of sheets. On rainy days and in winter the folding wooden clothes-horse would be out, and the whole house would be draped with damp washing. To my shame, I think I may sometimes have complained about the inconvenience. Mum did the ironing using two small cast iron flat-irons, heated in the oven or on the range, one in use while the second heated up. By the early fifties, she had an electric iron, but there was no washing machine until 1960, when Mum finally acquired a second-hand twin-tub, and her joy knew no bounds.

As Monday was always washday, so Friday was always bath-night. I can remember no exceptions to this rule. The copper was pressed into use once again straight after tea. The zinc bath was unhooked from the wall on the cellar steps and installed in front of the fireplace. I was first in the queue and had the privilege of clean water. Mum came next, while Dad dried me off, and the clothes horse was draped with a sheet and used as a screen to protect her modesty, which she always guarded jealously. I only once accidentally caught the briefest of glimpses of forbidden areas of her body, an experience that I found both surprising and disconcerting. Dad was third in line, not always with the benefit of the clothes horse screen. We all used the same water, although sporadically it would be warmed up a little using

---

[19] *Very few men's shirts with attached collars were available. Shirts often came with two sets of collars and cuffs, both of which quickly became dirty in Sheffield, even if you were an office worker, because of the atrocious air pollution. These accessories were attached by cufflinks or studs and a collar stud, which was literally and figuratively a pain in the neck. Collars and cuffs were the first part of the shirt to wear out, and so it was also an economy measure to replace them instead of buying a new shirt.*

kettles of boiling water. From the age of eleven, now at secondary school, I was released from the Friday night bath routine by my regular access to showers after PE, swimming lessons, games afternoons and Saturday matches, and Mum could bathe in clean water once again.

To the right of the chimney breast were built-in cupboards, floor to ceiling. The top section of the cupboard held crockery, cutlery, kitchenware and dry goods. The 'bottom cupboard' stored shoe-polish brushes, tools and hardware. It also housed the invaluable cast-iron hobbing-foot, which Mum and Dad used to cobble shoes, resole them or hammer segs into the heels. Beside the cupboards was the door leading to stone steps down to the coal-cellar that also served as our refrigerator. At the top of the steps was the indispensable cellar-head, a square cold space with floor-to-ceiling shelving for storing tinned food and perishables like milk, butter, lard and cheese.

In the middle of the kitchen stood an oak-veneered table, three-foot square, with leaves that extended it to five foot long if we had company. There were four dining chairs. Against the back wall was a matching sideboard. I still use the table and chairs to this day, in my own kitchen. My parents paid 30 bob for the set when they married in 1937. They borrowed the 30 bob from my Uncle Harry.

On a high shelf just inside the back door, in a polished walnut casing, was the wireless set whose dial promised exotic places such as Hilversum, Luxembourg, Kaludenberg, and Stuttgart, alongside less glamorous places like Daventry and Droitwich. The kitchen was lit by a central lightbulb and shade. There were no standard lamps or table lamps, there being little room – or money to spare – for such fripperies.

The front room, or as we called it 'the room', was little used, and I remember it as always being freezing cold when I was sent through to fetch the post in the mornings. It had a bay window, with lace curtains of course, and looked out onto Northcote Road. It had an oblong, patterned carpet over the lino in front of the tiled fireplace, surrounded by a three-piece suite in brown faux leather, which I considered the acme of luxury and comfort, and a posh looking china-cabinet containing my dad's cricket cups and the best china, for use only on very special occasions. Most homes had a pouffe, called a tuffet or buffet in Sheffield, but we did not. The room too was used only on very special occasions, such as Christmas, New Year and my birthday. On these festive days the fire was lit and banked up, lending the room a warmth that was as much emotional as physical. I believe the Danes call it *hygge*. Sitting snug in one of those armchairs, I felt like a prince.

A straight central staircase with 13 steps led to the two first-floor bedrooms. On the right of the landing, above the front room, was my parents' room, as chilly as a butcher's cold-room, because of its position directly above the unheated front room. I remember a high double bed, a wardrobe, a dressing table and a chest of drawers that still now serves as my stationery cupboard. On the other side of the landing, a couple of feet narrower than my parents' bedroom, was my room, above the kitchen and always cosy and welcoming, even in the depth of winter, although the windows did freeze up on the inside on winter's nights, acquiring a thick layer of frost or ice, into which I could inscribe secret messages to the outside world. I had a three-quarter sized bed, covered with a sheet, a scratchy wool blanket and an eiderdown. Duvets were unheard of. There was a wardrobe and a tallboy, and mother-of-pearl pictures on the walls. I was a lucky lad to have such a room to myself. I shall not elaborate on the 'gusunder', the 'jerry', or 'jemima' discreetly stowed under the beds, except to say that it was a long trek to the outside lavatory on a cold winter's night.

Leading from the landing outside my bedroom was the twisting, creaking, narrow staircase leading to the attic. There, for as long as I remember, stood my snooker table, tiny at only five foot long, with balls, pockets and cues scaled down to size, but with an authentic green baize-covered slate bed. From being too short to reach the playing surface without standing on Dad's tool-box, I spent hours playing snooker and billiards with my mum, who must have had the patience of a saint. I still have the table, the set of balls, cues, scoreboard and the original cue-chalks, although I confess that the base and the legs were long ago converted into a workbench and then prodigally abandoned, in 1969, in the garage of a house in Chancet Wood Close.

For the whole of my childhood, we always had a cat. My first cat, Tim, was a kitten when I was a baby and we grew up together for the first ten years of my life. Tim was a tabby with an infinite capacity for patience and tolerance. However much I petted and poked him or carried him round like a teddy bear, he never scratched or bit. He was my constant companion in my tent under the dining table with a tablecloth draped over it. Tim disappeared when I was ten, and a new kitten was presented to me as his replacement. I was pretty cut up about losing Tim, but the tiny new jet-black creature was a huge consolation. I named him Barney.

When we had had Barney for a couple of weeks, my mum sent me off with him to the vet's to have him 'doctored', whatever that was. I only knew that it was something that had to happen to all baby cats before they were allowed to be pets. 'Doctoring' kittens was performed free of charge at the PDSA in Napier Street. The vet's assistant took Barney away and then brought him back almost immediately with the news that the vet could not doctor him, as he was a little girl cat. My mother thought that this was hilarious, but then turned very serious and told me that we would not be able to keep Barney, and he would have to go to another family to be looked after. This after I had suffered so much before switching my allegiance from Tim! I was fit to be tied! Mum told me to stop showing off and promised a further replacement. The following week, Barney's substitute arrived, almost a replica of the original Tim, and so I christened him Tim also. The new Tim lasted a year before, according to the vet, he swallowed poison. I was done with cats. They were too painful.

A few weeks later, my dad came home carrying a budgie in a shoebox. He was followed into the house by a workmate, a shifty-looking chap called Whifty, bearing a budgie cage. This was my new pet, to be called Micky. Micky turned out to be a brilliant acquisition, hugely entertaining and very tame. We let him fly free around the kitchen. He was a great imitator, and I kid you not, he developed a small but impressive repertoire. 'Where's John?' was his favourite phrase and reinforced my theory that I was the centre of the universe. He could also say 'Micky Foster, sixxxteeeeeen Northcote Road' and did so over and over again, thus allaying any fears I had that he might fly away and get lost. When we had been away on our annual holiday to Bridlington and left Micky in the care of Mrs Woodhouse, he had even taken on her more pronounced Sheffield accent and started to say 'wheer's John?' and 'Northcut Roo-ad' instead.

There were some narrow escapes with Micky, but fortunately his ability to reel off his name and address to the police, if he got lost, was never actually tested. He liked to land on my shoulder and accompany me around the house. I put this down to his intelligent curiosity and, of course, to his loyalty and affection for me. I was, after all, the centre of the universe. One day, Mum sent me on an errand, and I had already reached the end of Carrfield Lane when I heard the familiar refrain: 'Micky Foster, sixxxteeeeeen Northcote Road'! I froze, turned slowly and walked back home, very careful not to disturb him or alarm him into flying off. Fortunately, we met no dogs or cats on our way back, and I locked Micky safely back in his cage. Micky lived on long and healthy, for as long as budgies live, and died, peacefully in the night, still knowing his own name and address.

Dad's workmate Whifty had also been the supplier of the piano which was to occupy a good deal of my free time from the ages of eight to twelve. As with any dealings with Whifty, there was some drama before the deal was concluded satisfactorily. The first piano that Whifty sold Dad for £30 was deemed to be unfit for purpose by the piano tuner, who told my mum that we had been robbed. Whifty was suitably apologetic, and a second, this time excellent piano had appeared in the front room when I came home from school the following Monday. The piano tuner declared it to be a 'snip' at £30.

I was to have lessons with Miss Rowley on Rushdale Road, at half a crown per half hour lesson, also thought to be a bargain, as Miss Rowley was said by my Auntie Eva to be a very good teacher. Eva's daughter, June, had been tutored by Miss Rowley and was a brilliant pianist. June was five years older than I, and I looked up to her as my clever older cousin, who was pretty and spoke with a posh accent because she went to High Storrs Girls' Grammar School. My mum and Auntie Annie had looked after her a good deal as a youngster, and so I knew her quite well, and I liked her. Her dad, my Uncle Tom, was in the army and spent the war years in Burma, without once coming home on leave, all of which made life hard for Auntie Eva.

Eva, June, Grandma 1941

From left, June, Mum, Alice, Annie, me (in pram) 1940

I soldiered on for four years at the keyboard under Miss Rowley's tutelage and appeared in several of her annual celebratory concerts, usually playing a nervous duet on a disturbingly alien stage with some girl I didn't know. I practised well enough, was competent and passed several grade exams, but with merit rather than distinction, a grading which, despite the congratulations of all my entourage, seriously damaged my amour-propre. However, Miss Rowley was a dull, dull teacher and my heart was not in it. My dad had said repeatedly that I should have gone to 'syncopation', instead of Miss Rowley's formal schooling, but this had only produced a frown from Mum, and I had no idea what he meant. When I gave up after four years, by now a faultless performer of the chromatic scale and capable of playing Beethoven's *Für Elise* with no little elan, Dad said: 'He should have gone to syncopation'. I am still not certain what he meant. Jazz style, ragtime? I should have asked, shouldn't I?

Having a piano in the house revealed a new side to my mum. She sometimes invited a neighbour of Auntie Annie and Uncle Ron, whom they always called Mr Storey and never by his first name, to come and play the piano for her. Mr Storey was a very gracious and polite, but very tall, very bald and very ugly man, with a gigantic nose that sprouted luxuriant black nostril hair. He also had large, bony-knuckled, clumsy-looking hands, which seemed unsuitable for piano-playing. He played very loud classical music, for two solid hours, with liberal use of the foot pedal and great flourishes of the hands, pausing only occasionally to sip his tea. I was totally intimidated by the sheer bravura of his recitals. I can only speculate what the neighbours thought of it all, but my mum almost swooned with delight at the sounds that our £30 upright piano was making. She always thanked Mr Storey a little too profusely, I thought, as he was clearly enjoying himself and only too pleased to be there. Perhaps it should have been Mum who had the half-crown piano lessons. She would have loved it, I think.

Our neighbours were a mixed bunch. Our next-door neighbours were the Kendalls, Marina and Tom, daughter Elsie, and their sons Jack and Les, the latter also called Scodger. Jack was grown-up, in the army and therefore remote, but I remember him as always very smart and polite.

As to Scodger, who would have been in his mid-teens, I recall him asking me if I liked tarts and me answering that I preferred lemon tarts to jam tarts. He explained that he meant girls, and even at my tender age I knew that this was disrespectful and vowed never to use the word. I often heard the word used casually, simply to mean girls rather than in its strict sense, but even so it reflected attitudes to women at the time. Happily, the usage of the term had pretty much disappeared by the time I was a teenager.

Mrs Kendall, whom her husband called Rina (rhyming with miner), was afflicted by a constantly anxious demeanour, whilst her husband Tom was a bluff, barrel-bellied, bald man who wore a broad leather belt underneath his embonpoint. The Kendalls kept chickens in a large square compound in the centre of the yard. Either Mr or Mrs Kendall quite often took me as a small child into the chicken coop to feed the hens. I was ambivalent about this privilege, encouraged as I was by my mum to have this exciting experience, but always relieved to come out unscathed. I was a pusillanimous little boy, the sort of child who doesn't like to be pushed too high on the swings. The chickens were a shabby-looking lot, perhaps one of the causes of Mrs Kendall's anxiety, and they seemed to squabble and peck each other quite a lot. My mother loved to tell the story of Tom Kendall saying to Rina: 'th'ad better wring that 'en's neck, Rina, afoor it dees, else wissal not be able to eyt it'[20]. A pragmatic approach to poultry husbandry.

Another great anxiety for Mrs Kendall that is worth remarking on is her great fear of kincough, which she expressed every time she saw me sitting on the back step: "Get off that cold step, you'll get kincough!' She often added, shaking her head, 'Well, I don't know, t' young uns'. Eventually, I asked my mum what kincough was, and she just laughed and told me it was piles. What was piles? Something older people got wrong with them in their bottoms. I

---

[20] *You had better wring that hen's neck, Rina, before it dies, or we shall not be able to eat it.*

decided it was nothing to worry about.[21] What *was* worth worrying about, however, was The Fever, which you could catch from playing too near the drains. Originally, the Fever most likely meant cholera, but now seemed to include diphtheria, scarlet fever and typhoid. If you caught any of these you were incarcerated in the dreaded Fever Hospital (Lodge Moor Isolation Hospital), where no-one could visit, and the only news of your welfare was printed anonymously on the back of the *Star*, alongside your code number. Scary! I confess that I did have the odd bad dream about the Fever Hospital.

But I digress, and so back to the Kendalls! Elsie, the eldest of the three offspring, was a nursing sister, with all the air of brisk efficiency and no-nonsense which seems to go with the office. She was a substantial woman, in physique almost exactly similar to Nurse Gladys Emmanuel of *Open All Hours* fame, or Hattie Jacques in *Carry on Matron*. I have noted that senior nurses often seem to have the large frame and endomorph soma-type of Gladys and Hattie. Whilst I am sure that it is not seen as a qualification for promotion in the nursing profession, their bulk does give them a distinct air of solidity and reliability, and is for once in their lives an advantage rather than a curse. The senior practice nurse at my own GP's surgery is similarly generously proportioned, and I am very fond of her and trust her completely.

At number 20, the end house in the yard, which had an off-shot kitchen and was the mirror image of my grandma's house at number 10, there lived Mrs Woodhouse, a short old lady who suffered badly from arthritis, found walking extremely difficult and appeared to limp on both legs. There had been a Mr Woodhouse, but he had disappeared from the yard, and I assume he had died. Mrs Woodhouse was swaddled in many layers of clothing at all seasons of the year and always had on the same shawl as a final layer. She was very amiable, constantly smiling and usually to be found in a rocking chair in front of the fire. Mum often sent

---

[21] *What Mrs Kendall almost certainly meant by kincough (or kinkcough, or kingcough) was whooping cough, a childhood disease which could be fatal.*

me to 'see how Mrs Woodhouse was doing', and this never felt like a chore, as she always welcomed me warmly with a biscuit. It was quite common practice for Mrs Woodhouse to call on us also, without ceremony, if she needed something or just wanted a little company. She would give just one knock on the back door, hobble in and sit on the chair beside the sideboard. Back doors were never locked, except at bedtime. 'Come in, t' door's on t' sneck'[22] was often heard. Mrs Woodhouse and her husband had been aficionados of the Sport of Kings when they were younger. She still 'studied form', circled the horses she fancied in the newspaper listings, and then listened on her wireless for the results. Sometimes, if she had a hot tip, she would arrive at our back door with a shilling folded up tightly in a scrap of paper, with *Monty's Dream,* 2.30 Ascot, *Mull of Kintyre,* 3.45 Lincoln, or similar written on it, and a request to 'get it on' for her.

In the next yard, at number 14, were the Pethers, including George, who was about my age, but went to a different school, and Mary, a year or so older. Mary was what my grandma called a bossy-britches and dictated which games we three played together. It was usually something involving film stars, guessing film stars' names from their initials or from our re-enactment of their part in a film. As I only knew Margaret Lockwood, Roy Rogers and Gene Autry, I did not feel fully engaged in these games, nevertheless I went along willingly, as I admired Mary's motherliness and authoritative manner. I remember George as playing a very much subordinate role, although he did sometimes cajole Mary into playing a game called Finger, Thumb and Rusty Bum, whose rules where never quite clear to me, but involved one of us making a back against a wall, as in leapfrog, and the others vaulting on top a set number of times, according to whether Finger, Thumb or Rusty Bum was guessed. I would imagine the game would have been more taxing with more than three of us playing.[23]

---

[22] *on t' sneck = closed but not locked.*

[23] *I discovered that this deliciously named game was played in playgrounds, between two teams, one team trying to force the other to collapse under their weight. I don't think I missed a treat.*

The two lived with their father and grandmother, who was totally blind and never ventured from the house to my knowledge. However quiet I tried to be, when I went into the Pether house, she always knew that I was there and exactly where I was, which was a little bit creepy. She did not wear dark glasses and had half closed eyes, revealing only the whites, all of which gave her the look of a character in a horror story. George and Mary's father was a mysterious figure, out at work all day and rarely appearing in the evening.

The Pethers moved away when I was about twelve and were replaced by John Quick and his elderly parents, who invited me to watch England's World Cup matches on their television. John shouted over the wall for me to come round for the final, Germany versus Hungary, who were the best team the world had ever seen, and who had recently thrashed England twice. By now, because I was learning the language, I thought of Germany, who were the underdogs, as my second team, and I knew all the players by name. They won 3-2, and the icing on my cake was seeing my favourite player, Helmut Rahn, score the winning goal. I could boast in German lessons that I had witnessed the so-called Miracle of Bern. Televised football is commonplace now, and during the Covid lockdowns there was scarcely a day without live matches, but at that time, even on a miniature screen in black and white, for a sport-mad boy like me, watching those world stars was the purest of magic, Aladdin's Wonderful Lamp and Sinbad's flying carpet rolled into one.

At number 12, the middle house in the neighbouring yard, lived Mrs Bower, who sported bright red lipstick, a thick layer of face powder and rouged cheeks at all times and owned an indeterminate number of cats. The most notorious of these was a tom called Figaro who constantly went missing, no doubt sowing his wild oats around Heeley. Mrs Bower stood on her doorstep every night before bedtime singing 'Figaro! Figaro! Figaro!' to the tune of an aria from *The Barber of Seville*. Figaro did usually slink home across the unkempt grassy area in the middle of the yard which constituted Mrs Bower's garden. She was either a widow, a spinster, or an abandoned woman and very much down at heel, as were the bedroom slippers that she wore not only to shuffle down to the lavatory but also to the shops. She never spoke, apart from to her cats, and seem to suffer the universal disapproval of all the women in the area, who rolled their eyes and looked to the heavens whenever her name was mentioned. Perhaps she was considered a slattern, perhaps she was still living down a disgraceful past. I never found out.

Across the lane from Mrs Bower's house were the Drews. Trevor Drew was a year younger than I, had prolific blonde, curly locks, and was a little chunky. More about Trevor I cannot relate. With apologies to Mr and Mrs Drew, I can only say that when I first saw Harry Enfield and Kathy Burke in their roles as Wayne and Waynetta, my thoughts instantly flew to our neighbours across the lane. The Drew family kept pigs in their backyard, an excellent contribution to the wartime economy, but a rather malodorous contribution. It was one of my few household chores, and I did not take a moment's pleasure from this task, to take across any vegetable peelings and tip them into the Drews' pig-swill bin. Trevor had an older sister, June, who made only perfunctory public appearances, and whom I remember as glamorous and rather more suggestive of a blonde relative of Tamara Drew than of her parents.

There are many more neighbours about whom I have only vague memories. One however, deserves a mention because of a kindness. Mrs Hines, who lived in the end corner yard opposite the Women's Guild, was older than my parents and had grown up children. She had a neat hairstyle and dressed smartly. I had always thought of her as a degree or two posher than us, although I had never had any dealings with her. One summer's day in 1950, while playing cricket in the lane, I hit the ball, a tennis ball, high and long. I was proud of the shot. It was my best ever. It arrowed towards Mrs Hines' kitchen window. I muttered a silent prayer, but to no avail. I heard the dreaded crash of breaking glass. I confess that my first response was cowardly. I ran home. After a few moments, Mum asked me what was up. I confessed.

What should I do?
Had I owned up?
No.

Where were the other boys?
Run off home.
Well, apologise and pay for the damage.
How? What with?
With money from your savings. Go now and own up.
How much would it be?
About seven and sixpence.
Would she come with me?
No. Go now.

I went to Mrs Hines' house, trembling with fear, clutching my money-box and key. I expected righteous rage. Mrs Hines came to the door. She was in the process of clearing up the mess of broken glass. I confessed, apologised, offered to help clear up, offered to pay for the repair. She politely refused my offers. It was ok. She had had boys herself.

I learned a lot that day, about life, about people, about myself. I leave you to decide exactly what.

None of these neighbours, in fact, as far as I recall, none of the people who lived on Northcote Road, not even in the posh houses, owned a car, and so those streets were completely free of parked vehicles. If we saw a car parked, then it was almost certain that someone was ill and the doctor had been called in. It is worth remarking that the family doctor did indeed make home visits in the 1940s and 1950s, an age when the very presence of a medical professional was thought to have healing properties. Doctors in those days were, of course, all male, would arrive in a great hurry, walk straight in through the front door without knocking – it was expected that the door would be unlocked in anticipation of his august visit – march upstairs to his sick patient's bedside, deploy his stethoscope, deliver his diagnosis and prescription for a cure, and march out again. At least, that was my experience.

Apart from the postman, of course, the other regular caller to the front door was the coalman, and this was because the coal grate was in front of the bay window in the front garden. When the coal lorry came, even from the age of three or four, I was deputed to count the number of sacks of coal that were emptied down the grate into the cellar. My mother simply did not trust the coalman, a suspicion perhaps born out of experience. The delivery was always one ton of coal, delivered in twenty sacks of one hundredweight. The coalman would prove to the customer that he had delivered twenty sacks by piling them next to the coal grate for the customer to count. It was my job, as delivery inspector, to ensure firstly that no already empty sacks were added to the pile, and secondly that no sacks were folded so that they were double-counted. I am fairly certain, from the way that the coalman glared at me through the bay window, that he knew that I was watching him with my beady little eye. Unfortunately, my beady little eye was not an X-ray eye and could not reassure my mum by discerning how much of the coal in the sacks was shiny black nuggets and how much was 'slack', another swindle often attributed to the shady coalman.

A second and crucial function of the coal-grate came into operation when we had locked ourselves out, which was easy to do and happened fairly frequently, as the back door was secured by a Yale lock. I would be dispatched down the coal-hole onto the pile of coal beneath and thence up the cellar steps to let the adults in, which made me feel important and useful.

Apart from the paper-lad who thrust the *Star* through the letter box, other regular callers would know to use the back door. The Co-op milkman, whom we never clapped eyes on, delivered the daily milk six days a week at the crack of dawn, in exchange for the Co-op milk tokens which were left on the step with the empty bottles. The insurance man called at intervals to collect the penny-a-week payments on the funeral policy. Twelve weeks was his usual interval, when he could collect a whole shilling.

The eggman became a regular caller from around 1950, for about three years. Every Saturday morning without fail, he would deliver half a dozen eggs to Mrs Woodhouse and then walk briskly, without knocking, into our kitchen, slip an egg into my mum's hand, lean over, wink, and whisper confidentially the exact same words: "Watch thi pen and be careful what tha signs." Mum was at a loss to explain this mysterious act of generosity. We learned to accept the eccentric eggman as philanthropic and perhaps a little mad. He stopped calling on us as suddenly and mysteriously as he had started.

We had a window cleaner for a while, but he was judged to be either unreliable or too expensive, and Mum reverted to sitting on the windowsill outside the bedroom windows, with her legs inside, clinging on by some mystifying magnetism whilst cleaning the outside panes with a window leather.

A fairly regular caller at the back door was the gypsy, offering lucky white heather and clothes pegs. Mum always bought some heather, as she thought it was good policy not to arouse the wrath of the gypsies, who were well known, she claimed, to put a curse on any house they took a dislike to. At any rate, Mum wasn't going to take the risk.

The ragman used to come up the lane about once a month, with his horse and cart, bellowing out his stentorian, but musical and rhythmic

'Any owd rags? Don . . . . kee stones!'

As far as I knew, the ragman was the only source of donkey-stones, which were a soft whiteish-grey stone, in the shape and size of a wedge of cheese, made up of something resembling pale cement, sometimes bearing the image of a donkey on one side. These stones were essential for the respectable exterior upkeep of the terraced house. Mum went through donkey stones at a rate of knots. They were used for presenting a well-kept back step and downstairs window sill. The step and window sill were first thoroughly scrubbed and rinsed (by the housewife, naturally), and then a white line an inch or more wide was drawn around their edges with the donkey stone. It was considered the height of slovenliness not to have a donkey-stoned back step. You didn't buy the donkey stone, but instead exchanged it with the ragman for discarded clothing, shoes, metal objects or furniture. The ragman was the recycler par excellence.

Finally, a word about the rent and tenancy of the house is perhaps of historical interest. Rent and tenancy of unfurnished houses was controlled by law, and as long as the tenant paid the rent on time, behaved respectably and kept the house in good order, the tenancy was secure. The repair of the fabric of the building was the responsibility of the landlord, the owner. As to our house in particular, and I have the rent books as evidence, my parents paid the rent on time every time, fortnightly in advance. Mrs Hastings collected the rent herself until March 18th, 1947, when she presumably retired, became indisposed, died, or decided to sell her properties. Subsequently, agents Cooper and Kinman collected the rent, which was 9s/5¾d (nine shillings and fivepence three-farthings per week) until June 1949, when the new owners, the Clegg Brothers took over. By April October1957, it had risen to 14s/2d, and when my mother left in 1966, she was paying £3.4s.6d every four weeks, 16s/1½d per week. The Cleggs, identical twins, were not excellent landlords and proved reluctant to repair their properties. My mother used to revel in stories she had read in the Star about the Cleggs avoiding prosecution for various crimes by mutually accusing each other and confusing the prosecution, a tactic identical twins have no doubt employed throughout the ages. I have no opinion on that matter and can only say that in any dealings I had with them personally I found them surly, laconic and unresponsive.

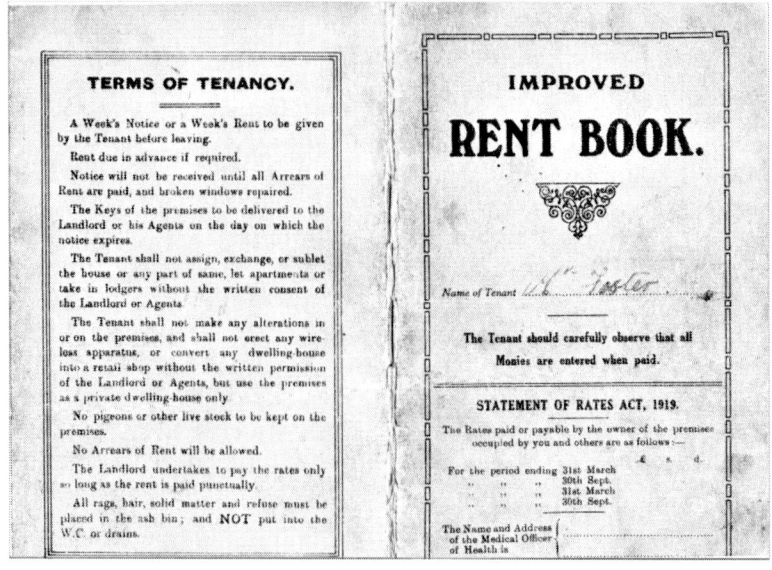

First rent book for 16 Northcote Road, 1937

V Shopping with Mum

Mum and I did the weekly shopping at t' Stores[24], the accepted name for the Co-op in those times in those parts. The Co-op still stands to this day in the very same building between Carrfield Lane and Carrfield Road, although its interior now feels claustrophobic and in no way reminiscent of the cavernous, high-ceilinged emporium I remember from my childhood. I can still recite the shopping list by heart – butter, sugar, marge, lard, flour, self-raising flour, eggs or powdered egg, bacon, cheese, tea, and milk tokens. Other items, like HP sauce, salt, vinegar, oats, jam, dried fruit were added as and when needed or permitted by rationing rules. Tinned tomatoes were a luxury, in the winter only, and only when the bottled supply of Dad's tomatoes grown in his greenhouse was exhausted. Later on, my mother would countenance none other than Cirio tomatoes as a replacement for Dad's produce.

We didn't browse in those days. We first of all stood in a long queue at one side of the shop to put in our order, which I was usually allowed to read from the list. One or other assistant – they tended to specialise – sliced the bacon on a machine, expertly scooped out or chopped off and weighed precise portions of flour, sugar, butter, cheese, et-

---

[24] *Usually pronounced stoo-ers, just as door was pronounced doo-er and floor was floo-er. Similarly road was roo-ad, and roar (used for weep) was roo-a, as in 't' babby's roo-arin' agee-an' (the baby's crying again).*

cetera, from mountainous blocks and gargantuan bins, and stowed them neatly in our shopping bag. Mum quoted her Co-op divi number, 62498, and handed over our ration books, buff coloured for her and Dad, green for me[25], along with the money, which was inserted along with a list of the prices into a metal container shaped like a four-inch dustbin. The container was attached to a kind of zip wire arrangement. The shop assistant then yanked on a lever and it sped up the wire like a tiny cable-car to a small windowed cubicle in an elevated position at the far side of the shop. There the cashier would take out the money, do the arithmetic, ring the appropriate total into the till, place the receipt and any change back into the metal container, screw on its cap and send it whizzing back down the return wire. Strangely, I did not wonder at the ritual aspect of this process. It was just how things were at t' Stores. When I was older, seven or eight, I sometimes did the weekly grocery shopping at the Co-op for Mrs Woodhouse, the old lady who lived in the corner of our yard. Her order was very simple and never varied – butter, marge, lard, sugar, flour, cheese, bacon, eggs, and seven milk tokens. I don't remember her divi number. She often gave me sixpence for my trouble.

There was, incidentally, another version of t' Stores, the S&E, the Sheffield and Ecclesall Co-op at the bottom of Ecclesall Road[26], this one not a grocery but a department store, called t' Arcade, where we went annually to buy my Whitsuntide clothes and later on my grammar school uniform. Once a year my mother collected her divi from the office at the S&E, a small percentage rebate of what she had spent over the year on groceries and clothes.

T' Stores butcher's was in a separate part of the Co-op building at the end of Carrfield Lane. I remember Mum creating ingenious dishes with limited ingredients such as ox-

---

[25] *Children under 5 had green ration books, as did pregnant women, while from the age of 5 to 16 children's ration books were blue. The differing allocations of coupons that they contained reflected the government's views on the food and clothing needs of the various groups of citizens.*

Clothes rationing ended in 1949, but food rationing remained until Summer 1954.

[26] *On the site of the current Waitrose supermarket.*

tail, cow-heel, and calf's head. Old habits die hard, and even as late as 1990 Mum was still making her wartime speciality, which she called brawn, a mysterious, wobbling dome of translucent jelly formed in a basin and suspiciously flecked with bits of meat from an unidentifiable part of an unknown quadruped. Brawn was carved off in wedge-shaped slices like cake and eaten for lunch or Sunday tea with salad. I was not a good eater and a constant worry to her on account of my anorexic tendency. Listing the food that I ate willingly takes very little time. I tolerated jam, rice pudding, Yorkshire pudding (or seasoned pudding[27]) with gravy, and bread and dripping, but only if the dripping had brown bits in it. Surprisingly, I was quite partial to a little stewed rabbit, as long as Mum had removed all the bothersome small bones before the dish was presented to the fastidious young prince. On the occasions when stewing beef was available, we would sometimes have beef stew, sometimes meat and potato pie. The beef stew, complete with other hated items like turnip, swede, celery and carrot, was the meal I hated most, but I did find my mum's meat and potato pie acceptable fare, as long as she had managed to remove all the gristle. The pie-crust and the potato marinated in gravy were the parts I liked, but a mouthful of gristle was liable to turn me bilious, make me down tools and refuse to eat another morsel. As I said, I was not a good eater. There were many times when the meat content of the meat and potato pie was minimal, and Mum would warn us by announcing, as we tucked in: 'If you find a bit of meat, shout "whip!".' As far as I was concerned, this was good news – the less meat I found, the better!

Other delicacies on offer included tins of corned beef and spam, the latter of which in our house was called 'premonition', 'prem' for short. I hated both and would only tackle them if they were accompanied by pickled cucumber and onions, piccalilli at a pinch. I occasionally resorted to native cunning to avoid eating undesirable food, for instance secreting it in my hanky or slipping it under the table to the cat. I remember one occasion when I was kept at the kitch-

---

[27] *Seasoned pudding was Yorkshire pudding with seasoning, sage and thyme I believe, and chopped onion added to the batter.*

en table for what seemed an age, but was probably no more than ten minutes, until I at least finished off my meat. I sneakily buried it in my mashed potato and was racked with guilt for days, a just punishment for my deceit. In any case, I was a rotten liar and my mum a top detective, and I am certain she would have seen straight through my duplicity.

Liver of all kinds also made relatively frequent appearances on our dinner plates, but always seemed to be riddled with a network of off-putting tubes, although its gravy at least was to my liking. I am aware that beef liver is reputedly the most nutritious of all foods, packed with protein, iron, minerals, vitamin B12 and goodness knows what other life-giving properties, but nowadays I wouldn't dream of tackling it.

I was even less keen on fish, possibly having been put off by the taste of canned snoek. The snoek was, I believe, imported from South Africa as an emergency wartime addition to our rations, but I think everyone hated it, not just I. A memorable moment of piscatorial horror in my early years was when I was persuaded, with the promise of unlimited salt and vinegar, to try whelks, which I had observed others swallowing with immense gusto. I vomited messily on the spot. My aversion to most sea-food remains to this day; the very thought of allowing a living oyster to slither down my throat is far more threatening than that of being waterboarded in Guantánamo. Only in my mid-forties, thanks to sun and sand and the beneficial glow imparted by chablis, did I grow to love *moules frites*. In certain circumstances.

Going to see the fish-man, however, was a different matter. As a nipper I had hair of the palest blond, practically white, and he would always greet me in his great booming voice with 'Look who's here! It's Blondie, my little bobby-dazzler!'

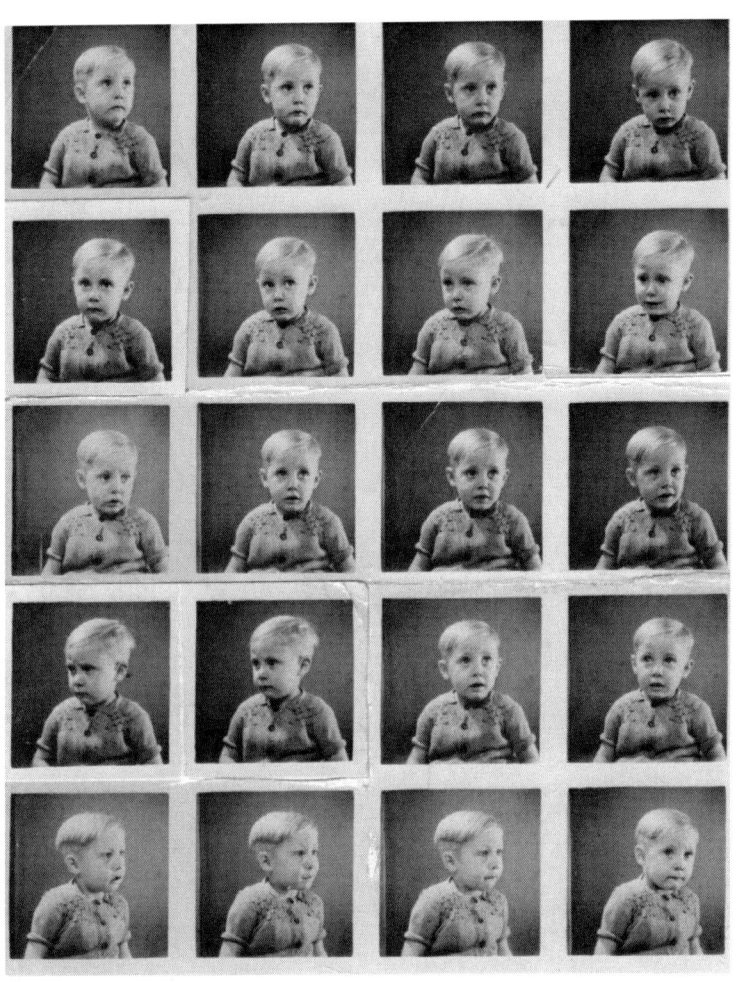

Blondie, the bobby-dazzler

Mum would hold me up for inspection, and the fishmonger would kiss me on the forehead and give me a silver sixpence. Already wise beyond my years in matters of thrift, I saved up these sixpences in the aforementioned money-box on the mantelpiece. Sadly, they and the money box disappeared long ago, along with my capacity for thrift.

I don't remember us ever eating chicken during my childhood, except perhaps at Christmas. I presume therefore that it was an expensive luxury at the time. I suspect that apart from liver the greatest source of protein for our family was the pork butcher's. This was not because we ate a lot of pork meat. Here my mum would buy tripe, chitterlings and bag. We ate the tripe and chitterlings just as they came – a quick rinse and onto the plate! None of that gross, slithery tripe and onions for us! The tripe was okay if you filled the holes with vinegar and added plenty of salt. I was and I confess still am a fan of salt and vinegar, neither of which I suspect is too good for my health. Chitterlings were a tender tube with a pleasantly tasting jelly within the its walls. I have no clear memory of bag, except that it both smelled and tasted revolting and I did not like it one bit. Fortunately, at the time I had no idea as to what any of these gastronomic delights actually were, anatomically, and I certainly could not stomach any of them now, if you'll pardon the pun. Sausages too were often available at the pork butcher's, but only the Good Lord and the pork butcher had any idea what they contained, and even they weren't too sure. One particular kind of sausage that I did like was polony, which you could spread on bread with a dab of mustard or piccalilli, for tea. It was bland enough not to offend even my finnicky tastebuds. Today I looked it up on the Internet to check what it theoretically contains. I can confidently assert that 1940s Heeley Green polony was, to say the least, unorthodox. It bore no resemblance to the bologna sausage or the American boloney that are supposed to be its equivalents.

As a sort of background music to mealtimes, I should add that although my own home and those of my large extended family of aunts, uncles and cousins were hardly palatial and our ancestry far from bourgeois, mealtimes were rather more formal than you might expect. We were required to use our cutlery properly, balancing peas on the back of a fork for instance, instead of using it as a shovel. Quite a difficult art, this, and one I abandoned in my teens upon realising its true absurdity. Eating with our mouth open to reveal its contents, speaking with our mouth full, or resting our elbows on the table were all strictly proscribed. Crossing knives was the worst sin of all, as it would inevitably cause friction and heinous strife in the family. At the age when I was beginning to become a little too big for my boots, I tried crossing two table knives whilst waiting for dinner to be served. I wanted to see what happened. I never saw my father so angry before or since. To this day, I still never knowingly cross two knives. Finally, we were not allowed to leave the table unless we had asked and received permission.

'I've finished. Please may I leave the table?'

'You may.'

There was a host of small shops in the Heeley Green area, among them a draper's, a sweet shop, a chemist, a greengrocer, a tiny tobacconist which sold pipes and tiny packets of five tiny cigarettes for apprentice juvenile smokers, a post office, a large grocer's shop called Bullace's opposite the picture house - a rival to t' Stores, I suppose, although we did not patronise it - and a mysterious shop run by the exotically named Aubrey Langhorne, which never had any customers. Aubrey was dapper, polite and single and seemed unaccountably to be the object of ridicule and name-calling from some boys. Looking back, I guess he may have been gay and therefore an outsider, poor man.

Strangely, there was no baker's, and even as a tiny boy I was deputed to fetch the daily bread from Memmott's on the corner of Fitzroy Road. Memmott's sold Gunstone's, our preferred loaf, which cost fourpence ha'penny, and I remember how I clutched the coppers very tightly on the long outward journey of at least a hundred yards, conscious of the responsibility. The return home was always more relaxed, as I was a dilly-dallier and an absent-minded nibbler of the crusty part of the warm bread. I suspect this was Mum's motivation for sending me on the errand, as I was likely to take in a little sustenance at least. I didn't mind running this particular errand, because, in addition to my licence to nibble, the Memmotts were nice people, and Mrs Memmott always had a smile and a kind word for me. They invented the flookypop, an ice lolly on a stick, which cost a penny. If the stick was revealed to bear the word flookypop printed on it, then you could return it and get another lolly free of charge. Often in moments of desperation, I would search the gutters of Fitzroy Road and Northcote Road for wantonly discarded qualifying sticks. It was my version of Willy Wonka's Golden Ticket. The Memmotts always honoured the flookypop stick, no matter how filthy a state it was in, or how faded the printing.

Another handy corner shop was Mrs Ashby's, close by at the junction of Northcote Road and Gleadless Road. Mrs Ashby's was where I went on Sunday mornings to fetch the Tizer, a delicious red fizzy drink, for Sunday dinner. Occasionally, in the interests of 'having a change', I was sent for Ice Cream Soda, pink with a sickly perfume, or Dandelion and Burdock, a dark brown potion with a slightly medicinal flavour, neither of which I liked much but tolerated if Tizer was unavailable. Mrs Ashby's outstanding characteristic was her fabled generosity, accidental or on purpose, in the matter of weighing boiled ham - Mum suspected she was short-sighted and misread the scales, whereas I judged her to be merely kind. I would be sent to fetch a quarter of boiled ham or potted meat (and often a gill of vinegar) and come home with half a pound or so for the same price. This was a refreshing change from stories of shady shopkeepers reputed to tip the scales with a sly finger.

At the end of Northcote Road, opposite Mrs Ashby's corner shop, was the fish and chip shop, or chip shop, as we called it. A portion of chips was threepence, as was a scallop, which was, surprisingly, a battered and deep-fried slice of potato rather than the marine bivalve mollusc you might quite reasonably expect. Fishcakes were sixpence and consisted of two slices of potato with a stingy allocation of flaked fish scattered in between, the whole thing covered in batter and deep-fried. Fish were ninepence or a shilling. Along with this feast, you could include a portion of peas, which were of course the familiar, northern mushy peas rather than petits pois. Chips and fish (in my case chips and a 'cake) provided a grand meal, was considered healthy enough, and most families could afford to buy them in for tea once a week, as a treat. They were served on a piece of greaseproof paper and wrapped in newspaper.

There was no curry sauce or gravy nonsense, none of your deep-fried sausages and kebabs hogwash, but, if you asked nicely, you might get some free scraps, which were scrapings of batter that had fallen off the fried fish, fishcakes and scallops during frying, had been rescued from the oil and dumped in a side compartment for consigning to the refuse.

As far as I know, people don't now generally beg for scraps in Sheffield. Perhaps I don't go to the right chip shops. However, earlier this year I was in Saltburn-by-the-Sea and bought fish and chips from a shop which appeared to be popular with the locals. Without exception, the customers asked for scraps, a sure sign of the poverty that has such a firm grip in the north-east, in towns like Middlesbrough, Redcar, and Newcastle.

In the yard behind the chip shop lived Jack Warriss, who ran an undercover hairdressing operation in his back room. I say undercover, because any visit to Jack Warriss was conducted in an extremely hush-hush manner, with much looking round and over your shoulder, presumably for a policeman or for anyone who might be mean enough to snitch to a policeman. Dad always took the torch with us to light our way through Jack's back yard. He would then tap lightly three times on the door, which seemed to be the correct signal to be let in, as the door would open a crack and we would be inspected for our bona fides. Possibly Jack was a barber by profession, worked in the daytime in a regular manner, and this was moonlighting. Possibly, Jack couldn't afford to rent premises or couldn't find premises to rent. I was between three and seven years old during the Jack Warriss era and was blissfully unaware that jiggery-pokery existed in the world, and so any commentary by me would be pure speculation. I do have clear memories of a lot of men all wearing flat caps or holding them on their lap, sitting all the way round the room waiting to be shorn. My conclusion is that it was cheaper than a regular barber's shop.

When it came to my turn, a board was placed across the arms of the barber's chair and I was perched on it. I was an unwilling customer and so Jack wasted no time. The clippers went straight into action, the haircut was over in a jiffy, my freshly cut hair was singed, using a wax taper, then squirted with fine spray of water, perhaps to put out the flames. This last operation was the bit I hated most, as the smell of burning hair always made me feel a bit sick and made my eyes water. At least, when I got back home, mum always said I was a brave soldier. Nevertheless, these visits to Jack Warriss recurred far too frequently for my liking.

I remember legion visits to the small local hardware shop, which always had a queue of customers blocking the way to the counter and reducing to a minimum any daylight that had managed to slip into the premises undetected. To say you could buy anything there is hardly an exaggeration, if it was of use in a house, yard or garden, that is. Nuts, screws, washers and bolts, et cetera were bought loose, usually by weight. Everything was stored behind the counter in dingy cupboards, ancient tubs and gloomy recesses. As well as hardware and ironmongery, advice about tricky household jobs was also dispensed by the wise hardwareman in the brown smock. It was a mistake to go to the hardware shop if you were in a hurry. You needed to set aside a couple of hours in your diary and plan your visit for a slack day.

Sadly, these idiosyncratic shops have largely disappeared, but I do know of a hardware shop in St Sulpice les Feuilles, France, which to this day maintains the traditional exacting standards of penumbral dinginess, long queues, crowds inside bigger than a Cowdenbeath home fixture, and wise counsel from a man in a brown smock. Please try it if you are passing. The cherry on this particular cake is that a hardware shop in France is called a *quincaillerie,* which somehow sounds exactly like what it is.

Another shop which warranted regular visits was Haining's chemist's shop, a few doors down from Woolhouses' newsagents. More than anything this was due to my tendency to ail with coughs, sore throats and head colds. Head colds and sinus infections were the curse of my childhood and adolescence and occasioned many a visit to Haining's. The chemist's was also the go-to shop for liquid paraffin and, surprisingly, olive oil, which was never used as salad dressing, as this was considered a disgusting foreign practice, but instead for earwax removal. Although Haining's had only a small area for its customers to wait, it had an extensive array of shelves full of mysterious items. I don't remember many of the names, except that I know you could buy concentrated sulfuric, hydrochloric and nitric acids[28] at the chemist's, as we once did to supplement my Christmas present of a chemistry set, when I was 11 or 12. Internet contributor[29] Brian Lee remembers seeing 'things like Syrup of Squills, Sweet Spirit of Nitre, Paragoric and Tincture of Myrrh', whatever they were!

Another reason for my frequent wintertime visits to Haining's the Chemist was my regular need for a shillingsworth of glycerine, opodeldoc and rosewater, a highly effective remedy for my chapped legs, caused mainly being obliged to wear short trousers at secondary school until I reached the fourth form.

Queueing at Haining's was done at the same level of hushed reverence as was customary in church whilst waiting for the vicar to speak. Orders often had to be whispered confidentially across the counter to preserve the modesty of the customer, who might be suffering from haemorrhoids, flatulence, thrush, or even warts. Condoms were, of course, not exclusively the domain of the chemist; they could, I understand, be obtained from the barber under the guise of 'something for the weekend', although probably not from Jack Wariss. This is hearsay rather than childhood memoir, and I have never experienced nor ever knowingly witnessed the purchase of said delicate items at either establishment.

Moving swiftly on to save us all further blushes, my ailing bronchial and nasal tubes are a good link for my visits to the doctor's surgery. People did not generally have telephones, and so there was not much of an appointments system, and patients were usually seen strictly in order of arrival. The doctor's surgery was on the ground floor of a terraced house. The wait to be seen often appeared interminable to me, and the small, stuffy waiting room, about the size of our front room, packed with sickly, coughing and spluttering patients cannot have been a very healthy environment. After the consultation, Mum would hand Dr McCallum a shilling in payment of his fee. Sometime

---

[28] *Under the archaic names of oil of vitriol, spirit of salt and aqua fortis, respectively.*

[29] *In Startsat60.news July 4, 2019*

around 1948 or 1949, I reminded her as we left the consulting room that she had forgotten to give the doctor his shilling. She told me that it was no longer necessary, as it was now free. The NHS had arrived.

My most frequent encounters with the health services were occasioned by problems at either end of the body, the feet and the teeth, and were at the 'School Clinic'. Lowfield Clinic was where I went on a fairly regular basis to have verrucas removed, painfully. I have almost managed to blank out of my memory these unpleasant consequences of my Saturday morning swims with Dad, Uncle Ron and Geoff at Heeley Baths, but I still have a clear memory of horrifically bloody tooth extractions, suffered unconscious under 'gas' at the terrifying Leopold Street Dental Clinic. My blood runs cold even now at the suggestion of a visit to Leopold Street.

The medical profession made several attempts to cure me of the common cold and blocked sinuses. The first of these was to cut out my tonsils, when I was four. When Mum informed me that I was to have my tonsils out and confessed to me that it might hurt for a while, I was naturally reluctant, as I had already heard rumours of this adult barbarity, but I was persuaded by my Uncle Ron's promise of lashings of ice cream in recompense. The dirty deed was done, and by some sorcery I was back home, fully awake in my bed at 16 Northcote Road, with a very sore throat. True to his word, Uncle Ron visited, found me in distress, hurried the half-mile to the nearest ice cream vendor on Forster Road, bought vast quantities of vanilla ice cream and then ran all the way back so that it would not melt before he arrived. Sadly, the ice cream was far too cold and my throat far too sore for me to gulp down more than a teaspoonful. I wept even more, and he and Mum had to eat it themselves.

This anecdote is just one illustration of Uncle Ron's kindness. I have not known a kinder man. He would go out of his way to help anyone and spent much of his time doing just that. He and Annie married on Christmas Eve, a couple of weeks before I was born, and my mum, heavily pregnant, catered for their wedding breakfast. The couple were close to me all my life and Annie was my favourite auntie, as I was her favourite nephew. Sadly, fun-loving

Annie was afflicted from mid-life onward with myriad anxieties and depressions. These were testing times for Ron also, but he retained his good nature and patience.

The most picturesque of the shopping opportunities in Heeley Green was the weekly market stall at the corner of Gleadless Road and Kent Road, run by a colourful fellow called Chopper – I think I remember the name correctly. He had a gravelly, stentorian voice, sales patter as entertaining as any cabaret act, and a delightfully idiosyncratic spelling technique. Sadly, I cannot remember any specific examples, but I do remember that it was strictly phonetic and apostrophes were scattered liberally and randomly and never in the right place. My favourite example of inventive spelling was presented to me by a teacher colleague in the 1980s. She showed me the word: YANETIN, found in an essay written by a third-year boy. Could I read it? I pondered long and hard, but was unable to come up with an answer. She gave me a clue: the boy was writing about rabbits that he kept in his backyard. I got it – wire netting! Ingenious. Chopper's spelling was like that. I wonder if they were related.

Wedding photo, Annie and Ron, 24th December, 1939

VI Sundays

My early memories of Sunday mornings are of my dad, dressed immaculately in suit and tie, taking me to see to his sister Kate and her husband Reuben in Well Road, where I would receive a right royal welcome that always set me marvelling at its warmth. They seemed good people, and I am sad not to have known them better. On the way, we would usually stop at Oak Street Church, where my dad spoke briefly with smiling elderly men and gave them a shilling, which contribution was entered in a ledger. This was the Friendly Society or the Mutual, I presume.

Most Sundays between April and September involved a family excursion into the Derbyshire countryside, usually a bus to Fox House and a day out on the Longshaw estate. We would set out fully loaded with haversacks bulging with provisions, waterproofs, Primus stove, methylated spirit, balls, and something to sit on, the grass being invariably wet. I carried the cricket bat and stumps, my share of the portering duties, with a certain air of *fin de siècle* resignation. Ever-presents on these expeditions were Auntie Annie, Uncle Ron and my cousin Geoff, five years younger than I. We were often joined by the Myers, Auntie Alice and Uncle George, from the more prosperous wing of the family, who would arrive by motorcycle and sidecar.

The mashing of the tea was the major preoccupation of the adults before the packed lunch, or dinner as we called it. I often felt a tinge of disappointment with Dad for allowing Uncle George to take charge of boiling the water on what was *our* Primus stove, but on reflection this seems to have been a shrewd move on his part, as the painfully lengthy process required ceaseless supervision, admittedly with the help of unstinting advice from Mum and Auntie Alice, frequent genuflection and at least half a box of matches to light and relight the flame, which blew out at the slightest provocation. Uncle George would inevitably end up complaining of stiff knees and reeking of methylated spirit. Nevertheless, it was accepted wisdom that tea made with spring water boiled on the spot on the Primus was far superior to tea which had stewed for a couple of hours in a thermos flask. I was glad not to share the adults' addiction to the national drink and perfectly happy with my allocation of weak Robinson's lemon barley water.

By now it was dinnertime and in the fresh, oxygen-rich Derbyshire air even I was feeling a little peckish. The packing-up was predictably 'prem' sandwiches, or cheese and tomato, or if we were very lucky boiled ham sandwiches with Colman's mustard, which helped to counteract the unmistakeable hint of methylated spirit. Even now, at the rare moments when I catch the smell of meths, my thoughts dart straight back to packed lunches at Longshaw.

I always set out on these Sunday expeditions in the hope that there would be cricket, but at Longshaw there was only one minuscule flat area suitable for play, on the far side of the stream where we pitched camp and ate our picnics. On sunny days this area would all too often be usurped by interlopers, and my afternoon's entertainment would be restricted to paddling in the stream and building dams with cousin Geoff, whom I regarded more as a little brother than a cousin. The two of us were always good pals, despite the wide age difference, and I secretly enjoyed messing about in the stream every bit as much as the cricket. On the rarer occasions when we took the bus to Baslow and walked into Chatsworth Park, there was always space and time for cricket, although finding a suitably flat, tussock-free pitch without cows or sheep in attendance was a challenge. As neither of my uncles was sporty and my dad was the only other competent cricketer in the party, the standard of play was not high, which was at times a frustration for me, the budding Len Hutton, on whom the humour of the spectacle was mostly wasted. My two aunties in particular were guaranteed to provide entertainment for the casual observer. My mother at least could catch well, but Auntie Annie, who excelled in energy, enthusiasm and giggling, was thoroughly incompetent and was teased mercilessly by Dad. As for Auntie Alice, whilst she could be relied upon to provide hilarious moments of pure farce, was half blind and, frankly, a liability to her team. Uncle Ron was a good sport, but Uncle George was always somewhat reluctant to participate, as he had once sprained an ankle so badly, when running for a quick single, that he been obliged to take a month off work. Such are the perils of amateur sporting pursuits. We were occasionally joined on these Sunday expeditions by the Pattersons, Auntie Lily, Uncle Don and their three boys, David, a few months older than I, Rob, a couple of years younger, and Jim, who was the same vintage as Geoff. These three lads added a distinct element of competitiveness and professionalism to the cricket games, with a great deal of attention to marking out the pitch, asking the umpire for middle and leg, looking round to check out the position of the fielders, frequent, vociferous appeals for LBW and run out, and subsequent earnest protestations of injustice from the disappointed party. These more serious games were equally enjoyable, but in a very different way, and I was more than a little miffed that I was no longer guaranteed to be the star performer.

On sunny days, a whole new dimension of entertainment was introduced into our Sunday trips to Chatsworth Park. Geoff and I would be bribed into the long walk uphill past the Huntingtower behind Chatsworth House with the promise of a swim in the lake. We must have both been hardier specimens in those days. Now, when I walk past the Chatsworth Lake, I wonder at my own foolhardiness and the rashness of our parents for allowing us to swim out into those freezing, murky, weed-ridden depths. The Duke of Devonshire even provided a diving board in those reckless days to encourage us to risk our lives! We dived in without a moment's hesitation, swam out fearlessly into the middle and loved every moment, until we turned blue with cold and were called in by our mothers.

Autumn and winter Sundays were less exciting. I still associate those Sundays with crushing and suffocating boredom, tempered only by the prospects of Yorkshire pudding and gravy accompanied on a good day by Tizer, *Family Favourites* and the *Billy Cotton Band Show*. Wakey-wakey indeed. The afternoon meant Sunday School at St Peter's across the road, bible stories and a spot of praying. I suppose these classes lasted barely an hour, but they seemed interminable. Whilst I was still in short trousers, I was press-ganged by a well-meaning Christian lady, whose name eludes me, to be a Sunday School teacher myself. I recall providentially few details, but I am certain that I was earnest and sustained the required degree of tedium. Other ingredients of the Sunday drudgery were the compulsory wearing of smarter clothes and the walk in the park. I could never understand the concept of the walk in the park, neither as a small boy nor later as a teenager, with The Girlfriend. I remember this aspect of being with The Girlfriend as the least rewarding area of the interaction with the opposite sex. But here I leap ahead too far. As a small boy I regarded the Sunday practice of walking with parents in the park as a grievous misuse of the facility, which should have been reserved exclusively for playing games. There was a tacit agreement, insinuated into our consciousness from the cradle, that enjoying yourself on a Sunday was sinful, and this included indulging in sport or any other activity which lacked the appropriate measure of solemnity. There was of course no professional sport and no cinema. We did not own a television set, although Auntie Alice and Uncle George did acquire a 9-inch model, from around 1951, and on our occasional Sunday evening visits we suffered *Muffin the Mule,* a puppet show of mind-numbing banality, therefore eminently suitable Sunday viewing, followed by a hypnotic and soporific 'short interlude' called *The Potter's Wheel*, but were then rewarded with the fascinating panel game *What's my Line.*

Ron and Dad, late 1940s

a rare whole family snap, years later

Sunday evenings at Auntie Eva's and Uncle Tom's always, invariably, as night follows day, followed their own, different pattern. Uncle George was the family pianist but had no piano at home, and so he was all too keen to tickle the ivories at any opportunity. The opportunity was our June's piano. After tea, out would come Uncle George's songbook, full of the favourites of the 20s, 30s and 40s. We always moved from beginning to end of the book in the same order of songs, so that whenever I now hear one of these songs draw to an end, the next one comes into my mind automatically and starts playing itself, an unwelcome earworm. Uncle George played each song at the same slow-medium paced, plinkety-plonkety tempo, no matter whether it was sad or jolly. He was consistent to a fault. The rest of us gathered round the piano, reading the lyrics from Uncle George's sheet music. I would gradually drift away from the group, musing about the exciting things I could be doing instead and wondering when the misery would ever end. One or two of the songs I didn't mind – *Pack up your troubles*, because it galloped along at a good lick, *Hold your hand out, you naughty boy*, because it was cheeky and hinted at an illicit love affair, *Oh! Oh! Antonio*, because it was funny and contained the ingenious 'left me on my ownio'. I particularly looked forward to *My old man said follow the van*, because it told a good story and had 'me old cock linnet' in it, which sounded a bit rude. But I loathed all the maudlin songs, like *If you were the only girl in the world* and *Roses of Picardy,* which were sung with especial enthusiasm by the womenfolk. *Now is the hour* was guaranteed to depress me every bit as effectively as *Oh God our help in ages past,* especially as Mum took every opportunity to make me sing it in company, either as a solo or a duet with her (even more embarrassing when it was at the Women's Guild).

Family Sunday evenings at Northcote Road were the most exciting, because on home turf I could generally lobby successfully for a game of cards. For money. By the time I was seven, I had become an inveterate gambler. The stakes were not high, ha'pennies and pennies, and my favourite game was *Last card Newmarket*. The stake was a penny per round, consisting of a ha'penny for the runner-out[30] kitty and a ha'penny for the last card kitty. The last card kitty was carried over to the next round if it was not won, and at a ha'penny per person per round, it could easily build up to a shilling or more, sometimes a bumper eighteen pence or two bob. It was won by the person who successfully played the king of the same suit as the hidden last card, to be revealed at the end of the round. As the kitty grew, my eyes became like saucers, and I was very alert to catch possible defaulters, like Auntie Alice in particular, who was notorious for forgetting to chuck in her two ha'pennies before each round. A bonus of these evenings was that Grandma could be there to join in the fun, as she lived close by and hadn't far to walk home. Grandma, like Auntie Alice, had her own special entertainment value. She could be practically guaranteed to hold, secreted behind another card or in plain view, the missing eight of clubs or jack of hearts, which had prevented the game from running its natural course and meant that the round had to be played out again from the beginning, sometimes frustrating a joyful winner of one of the jackpots. In this case, I would take on the role of adviser to Grandma, in other words looking at her hand whenever necessary. Of course, it goes without saying that I would never have dreamt of advising her to play a card advantageous to me. God's honour, as we used to say in the playground. I should add a final note here about the liberating effect of the motor vehicle. In the mid-50s Uncle Ron acquired Uncle George's old Ford saloon, and when he passed his driving test, at the third attempt (Don't go thinking you're Stirling Moss, said the examiner), Sunday afternoons changed for ever and became a time for exciting excursions to new places in the Peak District and the Dukeries. The Ford was no limousine. It struggled to climb hills, often having to be pushed, its radiator would boil frequently and then the flustered engine would demand a short restorative timeout in a layby. Most intriguingly, it had four foot-pedals, the customary accelerator, brake and clutch, plus a fourth pedal attached ingeniously to the gear-stick, which had to be held down to prevent it from jumping out of gear.

---

[30] *The one who played all the cards in his/her hand first.*

Grandma in her early 50s

Alice, Grandma, Lily, c1927

VII School days: Carfield

My first school was Carfield Infants on Argyle Road. I have only a few scattered memories and images, probably the traumatic parts of the time I spent there for the most part. I do remember going reluctantly and apprehensively with my mother to 'put my name down' for the school some weeks or months before I started, of feeling timorous and tiny in the face of this colossal stone building with so many windows and a bewildering network of corridors. My next memory is of the dread day when my mother abandoned me to the tender mercies of Miss Earnshaw, who installed me in my desk in the back corner of the classroom, seated next to a girl whose name I cannot recall. I know that Miss Earnshaw's mercies were tender enough, that she was kind and firm, and younger and prettier than my mum, with short, dark hair. I wonder what became of you, young, pretty Miss Earnshaw.

I remember practical music lessons and longing for a more interesting instrument than the tambourine or triangle to which I always seemed to be assigned. I remember a traumatic hearing test to which we were all submitted by the visiting school doctor, this in a different classroom and a recollection still so clear that I feel I could lead you today to the very seat in the very classroom. We all wore headphones and were asked to write down what we heard. Throughout the test I heard nothing but a hiss and a crackle and was convinced that I was deaf and condemned to be an outcast and unworthy in some way because of my deafness. I confessed my fears to my mum a few days and restless nights later when she quizzed me about what was bothering me. Of course, the fault was technical and not with my hearing, which was perfectly fine, but I was disappointed that I could not take the test again and show how well I could do. Failing a test was already unacceptable!

I remember nothing about the teaching methods in the school and so can contribute little or nothing to the history of pedagogy in post-war Sheffield. There are no eureka 'I-can-read-words-Mum' moments to relate. I can't even remember a time when I couldn't read or do simple arithmetic, although I don't imagine I was born literate and numerate. I do, however, remember with affection our English readers, stories of Old Lob and his farm. My favourite character was Percy the bad chick[31], but there were others that still stick in the memory – Mrs Cuddy, the cow, Willy, the pig, Mr Grumps, the goat, Mr Dan, the dog, and Dobbin, the horse. Aren't all horses called Dobbin? I presume that the *Old Lob* series was The Latest Thing in teaching reading and am grateful for it. I loved the stories and they were clearly light years ahead of the legendary *Janet and John* series, which I never had to suffer, thank goodness. One thing troubles me: I cannot remember a Mrs Lob. Sexism in children's readers in the 1940s? Surely not!

Mum took me to school again on the second morning, but from then on I was judged capable of walking there and

---

[31] *'I am Percy. I am a chick. I am a bad chick.'* How could I possibly forget such memorable lines?

back alone. *Autres temps, autres mœurs.* The walk probably took me fifteen or twenty minutes, unless I dilly-dallied more than usual. I measured the distance recently and found it was half a mile. I am certain it was further when I was five; it seemed another part of the world then. I didn't stay for school dinners, but came back home each day for the midday break. I can guess that Mum decided I wouldn't eat much anyway and the school dinner would not be value for money. Far better to make sure I ate something, however meagre, at home, where she could at least force a spoonful of malt and some welfare orange juice down me! It must have meant a quick turnaround at dinner-time, but I don't remember feeling rushed. Perhaps children have no concept of rush or 'hurry-up'. I think there were only two occasions when Mum regretted sending me out alone, and both incidents seem to have gone down in family history; I either remember them or remember being told about them multiple times. The first incident was when, aged five, I strolled home at dinner-time in a monsoon without my sou'wester on, whistling *Pedro the Fisherman,* and my mum and Auntie Annie became hysterical and tore off all my clothes ('every stitch!') and rubbed me vigorously with a towel. I was taken aback by all the commotion, amplified because I was ten minutes late, as I had been enjoying the soaking a good deal and consequently dilly-dallying more than usual. The second was a couple of weeks after my seventh birthday, during Britain's snowiest ever winter. Carrfield Lane and the gennels had become impassable overnight, blocked by drifts taller than me, and so Mum watched me set off from the top end of Carfield Road, heavily swaddled and wearing my cousin June's old wellies, picking my way through snow two foot deep with massive drifts. At about 100 yards, she related that I vanished completely into a mound of snow and did not emerge. She took pity on 'the poor little lamb' and stumbled through the arctic landscape to rescue me. She found me with my wellies full of snow, my hat already lost, and my face blue with cold. She decided that I should be subjected no further to the glacial conditions, not even in the sacred cause of education, and kept me at home for the whole day.

I remember the names of only two schoolmates from infant school days, and those only because our paths crossed once more at grammar school. Both were also called John – we Johns were legion in those days – John Anderson, taller and fair-haired, I remember because in subsequent years he was my constant rival in junior school for Number 1 spot in the ratings in annual school reports, and the shorter, curly-haired John Ashmore, with whom I maintained a loose but comfortable friendship until we were 13 or 14. He lived at Hollythorpe, about a mile from my house and I used to hang out with him there from time to time. He never came to mine. What happened then, I cannot say, but it ended. There was no falling out. Perhaps, as in the case of many friendships, one of you moves away, geographically or psychologically, or you simply find you have no further need of one another or interest in one another. Others you don't see for years on end but still consider yourselves firm and reliable friends. A very few remain friends for life, if you're lucky.

At the age of seven, I was moved to the Carfield Junior Annexe, much nearer to home, in fact at the end of our street. I remember my first day at junior school with embarrassment still. First of all, we arrived late, almost certainly owing to my needing to be persuaded and cajoled into risking my life entering this threatening new building which I had observed to be full of big, alien, scary children. Then, in front of a whole class of my peers and my new teacher, Mrs Jones, I humiliated myself. To my horror, my treacherous mother told the teacher that I would be taking school dinners and handed over some money to seal the deal. This betrayal and the misery of not going home at dinner-time was too much for me to bear, and I burst into tears and stamped my foot disgracefully. The deal was cancelled and the money returned, but I knew I had behaved badly and was wretched for the rest of the day.

After a couple of weeks, when I was settled into the school, had got to know my new classmates and found them to be not so bad after all, I realised that perhaps I was missing some fun not staying at school to play with them at dinner-time and decided to give school dinners a try. They were not appetising, not even for children who liked food. Another discouragement to my fragile appetite was the rhyme that mischievous pupils chanted before and even during school dinner:

Scab and matter custard, green phlegm pie,
All mixed up with a dead dog's eye,
Bogeys on toast, spread on thick,
All washed down with a cup of cold sick.

The dinners were delivered to the school hot, in large oblong metal containers, in time for dinner. Two permanent items on the menu were mashed potato and cabbage, and another stalwart was semolina pudding, occasionally substituted by sago pudding, which we called frog-spawn. The mashed potato, often pervaded by hard, uncooked lumps which tasted disagreeable, was nothing like my mum's mashed potato. The cabbage was limp, pale green and smelly, and merely removing the lid from one of the oblong containers of cabbage and releasing the pent-up aroma was enough to send the first 10 pupils in the dinner queue staggering backwards in shock from the assault on their olfactory receptors. There were often carrots and, far too often, minced turnip or swede. There was gravy, a glutinous, dark brown fluid which needed constant stirring to prevent it from congealing, delivered to our plate with a tin ladle, whether we wanted it or not. There was always meat and, on Fridays, fish of some type, with a white sauce. For dessert, there was the daily bonus of a spoonful of red Bolsover jam added to the pudding du jour, dispensed by Mrs Palfreyman, the buxom chief dinner lady. For me this was the highlight of the meal. I am not sure how much of this wholesome food I ate, but I know I did eat some, and I am grateful for it now. Along with the free milk at morning break, the orange juice, malt, and syrup of figs from the Welfare, the vitamins and minerals they provided, the vaccinations, the cheap and soon free healthcare, the admirable post-war Labour government ensured that we grow up strong and healthy. Thank you, Mr Attlee and friends. If only today's leaders had half your vision, altruism and integrity!

For the next four years I was in the same class of 34 children and so came to know them all well. The strange thing is that though our world was small and our horizons narrow, though I and most of them continued to live in the same houses, there were only half a dozen or so whose paths crossed with mine after we left junior school to disperse to our different secondary schools and blunder on into adolescence. I remember the rest still as they were then. A few spring to mind now. George Knowles and Kenneth Lawson I still think of as a pair, as I did then. George, a rugged-looking lad, always had inky fingers, as he was the boy who was appointed to the coveted office of inkwell monitor, possibly to get him 'onside' in modern parlance, as he was, I recall, not naturally inclined towards schoolwork. Kenneth's family had a small livestock farm a few streets above the school. He was the tallest boy in the class, fair-haired, broad-shouldered and angular. I remember him as slow to react and fairly pacific, but somehow or other he was one of the two boys in my whole life with whom I had anything resembling a fight. I have no recollection of the cause of the friction between us, but it was decided that there was only one way to resolve our issues. A fight was convened after school at the gate of the small farm in the lane alongside the playground. I can recall clearly the adrenaline and the fear, knowing I was certain to come off second best against such powerful opposition, but knowing also that it would have been worse to be considered yellow – 'yitten' in Heeley children's argot. Jackets held by our seconds, ringed by a small, expectant circle of spectators, we sized each other up, fists bunched, blood hot. I was rescued by a *deus ex machina* in the shape of an old lady returning home with her shopping, who told us to 'behave and not be so silly'. I have only at one other moment in my life felt such relief, three decades later, when Wednesday beat Southend 2-0 on the final day of the season to avoid relegation to Division 4.

Two other boys went together naturally because they were twins. Robert and Michael Gould lived a couple of streets away in Romney Road. We were good friends, perhaps because we all liked school. They were identical, but I had no problem differentiating between the two, even at a distance. Michael was the more confident, whereas Robert had a bit of a stammer. Their father was a white-collar worker, their mother well-spoken and polite, and I was always welcomed into their home, although I felt inhibited, as I knew they were one rung above me on the social ladder. They moved out of the area when the boys left junior school, but Michael and I went to the same grammar school, and although he and I were in the same class for German from the age of 13 to 18 and got on with each other well enough, we had little in common and were never what you might call friends. Regrettably, I remember seeing Robert again just once, briefly and accidentally, years later. I realise now that it was only he for whom I had felt an instinctive friendship.

Another two I think of together were the two Davids, Fielding and Moseley, who lived in a pair of semi-detached houses much further up Gleadless Road, opposite the daisy field. David Fielding was affable, placid, slim, blond and handsome, and later, as a teenager, I envied his good looks. In sharp contrast, David Moseley was burly, stammered, and was not so admired by the girls. He was normally good-natured enough, and we were always on friendly terms, but he was unpredictable and occasionally liable to fly into a volcanic rage with little or no apparent provocation. This, on account of his burly frame, made me wary of him.

Michael Storr sat on the opposite side of the classroom from me, under the street window, next to Brian South, of whom I have little recollection, except that schoolwork did not come easily to him. Michael was a nice enough lad, whose parents were much older than mine and were always charming, kind and generous. Sadly, Michael was afflicted with many of life's disadvantages. He had severe learning difficulties and a hare-lip that affected the shape of his face and made it difficult for him to speak clearly. I saw him again often in my teens and twenties, as he was a well-known local figure constantly walking around the area, smartly attired, with a cloth cap on and pipe clenched between his teeth, looking and acting like an old man. We would stop and hold short conversations, which to my discredit I found uncomfortable.

A few of the girls stand out. Vicki Cross, (yes, Victoria Cross, and I think her father's name was George!) like me an only child, sat either next to me or behind me at different times. Her father was a police inspector, and she was rather upmarket. They lived in one of the posh houses in the crescent at the far end of Fitzroy Road. Vicki was a tall girl, of substantial proportions, stately and well dressed, with a healthy complexion and tidy hair. She did not mix much with the *hoy polloi* in the playground or the lane, but, nevertheless, I felt we were friends and I admired her specialness. She was my principal rival for the accolade of Top of the

Class at the Annexe, but I always managed to fend off her threat to my hegemony. In her teens and adulthood, she quite probably became one of those intimidating, statuesque beauties who strike dread into the hearts of mere men. I shall never know, as we lost touch after junior school, and I never saw her again. On reflection I realise that, although we lived on neighbouring streets, our paths only ever crossed in the classroom.

Pamela Mills and Pat Howard always seemed to be close friends from the first moment I knew them. They were that common mix of extravert and introvert. Pam was shy and shared with me the curse of having to wear glasses from the age of about nine, which in my mind gave us an unattractive, geeky look. Pat Howard, was the lively one of the pair whom I found a little intimidating, even more so later, when in her teens she developed not only 'personality' but also a spectacular bosom. 'Personality' was something I realised I did not have and probably never would have. I was too shy, especially in those tactical skirmishes with the opposite sex. Pam and I remained friends until I disappeared to live in Ashby de la Zouch, but I haven't seen her since.

Pat Earnshaw and Maureen Mullins were two other girls that I remember clearly. Pat lived on Northcote Road also, about 20 yards on from the church. She had dark brown hair, in a pony tail, was pretty, and I 'liked' her. I do not, however, remember us ever having a conversation with each other throughout our childhood and teen years, although we smiled at each other quite a bit. She was probably shy too. Pat married Tommy Broomhead, her first boyfriend, who joined the police force after school and went on to become the Chief Constable. He was also the other boy I tussled with, when we were 14. I saw him about 10 years ago, and we recognised each other. He greeted me warmly, we shook hands, and I sent my regards to Pat. Neither of us mentioned the fight.

I 'liked' Maureen too. Again, I never spoke to her and I haven't even the faintest idea where she lived, but I did find the way that she danced in the lane at playtime attractive, and she seemed nice. Maureen was quite small, had short, brown hair and rosy cheeks; she was neat and pretty and appeared very clean. She never spoke to me as far as I remember, nor did she show the slightest interest in me. I 'liked' her from afar. Of course. Perhaps it's not too late, now that I am not quite so shy and have finally acquired a trace of 'personality'. Maureen, if you're free, give me a call. Perhaps we can still get it on.

Our daily routine remained similar throughout our time at the Annexe. After the ritual filling of the inkwells on each desk by George Knowles, often assisted by Kenneth, we always began the day with 'Mental'. For us, 'Mental' meant a mental arithmetic test of 30 questions read out by the teacher. We wrote only the answer to each question on a long slip of paper, or sometimes on our slates. The answers were then marked by our neighbour and checked by the teacher. We wrote with a pen which was simply a wooden stick with a replaceable nib. We dipped this primitive tool in the inkwell to prime it, being careful not to pick up so much ink that it would drop great blobs onto the paper. Inevitably there were blots and smudges, and for this we had blotting paper. If we made too much of a mess, we were scolded. We were only human for goodness sake! – have you tried using one of those school issue pens? Especially when its nib is bent or crossed. We recited and learned our times tables in chorus, did more sums, multiplications and long divisions, for example, then reading and writing, or composition. Our classroom in J1, J3 and J4, was one half of the main hall, a space which covered at least half of the building and had a huge central fireplace surrounded by an equally huge fireguard. The other three classrooms ranged around the perimeter of the building. Because our classroom was in the hall, which was used for school dinners, morning lessons ended 10 minutes earlier for us, so that the boys could set out the tables.

The afternoon would have different components, at times a little elementary geography or history, scripture studies in the form of bible stories, and some recreational stories read to us by the teacher at the end of the day. Very occasionally there was singing, although we had no piano, and so there was no accompaniment. Strangely, however deep I delve into my memory for even fleeting images of an assembly, I come up with nothing.

We practically never had anything remotely resembling a PE lesson, except for one or two occasions when we did a few 'physical jerks' in our vests and liberty bodices[32] out in the lane. However, on one afternoon per week those of us who could swim went off in a small group, unaccompanied, to Heeley Baths, a mile or more away, for our swimming lesson.

Morning and afternoon playtimes, about 15 minutes each, we could spend in the lane that ran uphill past the school, or in our playground further up the lane. The boys' urinal was a brick wall between the school and the playground, with a channel and a grate at the foot of it. There must have been a sit-down cubicle somewhere, probably indoors, but I don't remember ever using it. At dinnertime, the boys mostly played on the playground, which was a bomb-site, between the school and Denmark Road. It was hardly an official playground, but we knew no other and we used it as such. The remains of buildings had been demolished and the rubble cleared, leaving the outlines of the internal and external walls at ground level, a generously sized, flattish central area, where we played our semi-organised football games. There was a lot of clay, mud and puddles around, and the outlines of the building were a danger for the dashing, young footballers to trip on, as well as the further hazard of loose, broken half-bricks. At the top end of the yard was a steep earth bank, no good for football, but excellent for chasing round, playing tiggy and letting off steam.

When we were not playing football, we played marbles, or 'mabs' as we called it, competitively, for keeps. The clay surface provided us with ideal conditions for mabs. 'Oily' (South Yorkshire argot for Hole-y) was the preferred game. A neat, marble-sized hole was made in a flat area of earth, and each player rolled a marble as close to the hole as he could from a pre-agreed distance, generally about three paces. The

---

[32] *Liberty bodices took several forms: they could be simply a knitted, fleecy vest or one-piece underwear set, as worn by small children and slightly older girls. The liberty bodice was first intended for women, meant to replace the corset, and was usually a warm, one-piece undergarment with suspender straps. Some older women still wore the undergarment as late as the 1970s.*

nearest to the hole was first to play, and so on down the line. The first boy took all the marbles and rolled them together at the hole. He then attempted to nudge a marble at the hole with one finger. Any marble that went in the hole was his. His turn stopped when he missed. There were some simple rules. First of all, only certain types of marble were regarded as legitimate. We were allowed to play with 'globbies', which were similar to the regular glass alley, but oversized, about twice as big. 'Chippies' were chipped alleys and were legitimate if they were bigger than half-sized. In our school of thought, although not universally, steel ball-bearings were permitted so long as they were not rusty. 'Potties', pot marbles, were frowned upon and only allowed in friendly not-for-keeps games. 'Stonkies', made of some weird, lightweight substance, possibly chalk, were not allowed under any circumstances, and had no value. Globbies were, for obvious reasons, more difficult to hole, and some boys specialised in globbies. Other boys would have their own tricky chippy, whose trajectory they believed only they could control. You had to play the marble as it lay, even if it fell into a depression or behind a stone or root in the earth. You were however allowed to remove loose impediments, although I am sure we didn't use that phrase. Before each turn we had to utter the mantra 'conks, owts and everies'. 'Conks' was when one marble collided with another, perhaps on purpose, to knock it into the hole or to go 'in-off', as in billiards. I have no idea what 'owts and everies' were – possibly a nod to tradition, a throw-back to a forgotten age of more complex rules – but we had to say it nevertheless. If we wanted the right to swap our own special or favourite marble, should we lose it in the game, we had to say 'swaps, conks, owts and everies'. These rules were sacrosanct and there was no right of appeal.

As a beginner in J7, I was a poor competitor. I lost all the mabs that I had inherited, probably treasures from the childhood of uncles, and had to rely on my occasional spending money and the generosity of my dad, who would ask how I had fared and take pity on me, funding me the shilling I needed to buy more from Woolhouses' paper shop, the only known source. A packet of marbles was expensive, costing a shilling and containing originally eight and later, to my disappointment, only seven - an early example of exploitation of children. Mum made me a red velvet bag with a drawstring to keep my mabs in, but it was all too often empty. With time and practice I did become more proficient, and by the time I left the Annexe I had become practically a marbles magnate, even outplaying boys of my own age. There was one unpleasant aspect to marbles at the Annexe. Occasionally during a game, an unscrupulous or mischievous boy, even if not part of the game, would yell 'scrag your mabs', which was the signal for everyone to dive in and grab as many mabs as he could. It was every boy for himself, and I hated it. It was an introduction to the seamy side of life that we would meet later on, and for that training I suppose I should be grateful.

Another marbles game, to which I was less partial, was Ringy. A circle was drawn in the earth, or on the pavement, and boys each placed a marble in the circle. We took it in turns to flick a mab, from a standing position, with thumb and index finger, at the mabs in the circle. If we hit any and knocked them out, we won them. As I found I was incompetent at Ringy, I didn't enjoy the game and usually avoided playing it, whenever I could do so without losing face.

There were other, seasonal games. From autumn on, conkers was very popular. There are very few pleasures so easily obtained as gathering a bagful of shiny, new horse chestnuts. I loved to hold them, gaze at them, admire their perfection. I still do. It was almost a compensation for the loss of the summer and helped to sweeten the hateful damp autumn. However, although new conkers were more beautiful, they were usually less resistant and more easily split. Occasionally though, a new conker would prove to be special and win many battles. We used a gimlet, or in my case a red-hot skewer, to bore a hole through the horse chestnut, from top to bottom, and then threaded it onto a stout string about 18 inches long, with a strong knot in the end to prevent the conker from falling off. String length was a tactical decision. A longer string gave your strike more force but reduced accuracy, whereas shortening the string by winding it around your hand meant you were less likely to miss but rendered your strike less powerful. You held your string dangling perfectly still, at arm's length, from just above shoulder height, while your opponent was allowed one swing of his own conker to try to deal it a fatal blow. Then it was your turn to hit. If you broke an opponent's conker you accrued all its past victories and added them to yours. If, for example, your conker was a 7-er and you conquered[33] a 32-er, your conker became a 39-er. How to be competitive at conkers was a topic much pontificated upon by sapient greybeards, uncles, fathers and older boys who were veterans of the sport. It was regarded by many boys and their parents as legitimate to bake your conker in the oven, and some fools even advocated pickling it in vinegar. I was not a believer in either of these tactics; I regarded baking as unfair and pickling as plain daft, as I was sure that vinegar would just make the conker soggy. I was a great stickler for fairness in conkers, holding my conker very still to be struck by my opponent, and never deliberately 'jagging'. Jagging, which was strictly prohibited, was striking across diagonally so that your string snagged round the opponent's conker and dragged it down onto the knot of his string to split it. Top conkers often looked like battered old pugilists, being dried up and having lost all their shiny skin. I once retired a conker when it was looking in danger of disintegrating, in order to conserve its champion status, which I realised was, strictly speaking, rather cowardly, or at the very least dog-in-a-manger behaviour.

Whereas conkers definitely belong to the domain of boys, presumably for its atavistic machismo, there was one seasonal craze which was equally popular with both sexes. Indeed, girls were often far too good for us boys, owing to their superior manual dexterity. Fivestones arrived in Woolhouses' paper-shop one day and took the Annexe by storm. The fivestones that we came to know and love consisted of five little wooden cubes a little smaller than an Oxo cube, with four ridged sides and two flat sides. I understand from knowledge passed down to me from an older generation, may they rest in peace, that they would have considered our version of fivestones far too flimsy and lightweight for the job, in comparison with theirs in the good old days, when they were made of clay or chalk, and in many cases homemade. Ours were made of cheap, brightly coloured, lightweight softwood, and we modern generation didn't mind one

---

[33] *I believe the original name for the game was conquerors.*

bit. I am uncertain how we came to know this, probably again from tradition handed down from an omniscient older generation, but there was a series of routines that had to be completed in the correct order, consisting of throwing up, catching, manoeuvring and manipulating various numbers of stones[34].

From time to time there would be new 'crazes', as we termed them, and new playthings would appear in Woolhouses' paper-shop. Whips and tops were in vogue for a while, again a pastime at which girls excelled and which I found tiresome and derived no pleasure or satisfaction from, probably because I was useless at the game and didn't have the patience to practise something that didn't involve a ball and was therefore pointless.

The yoyo came bounding onto the Heeley Green scene around the same time as Pepsi-Cola, a delicious new fizzy drink, and both took the Annexe by storm. Pepsi-cola came in a snazzy small bottle with a crown cork and I remember being amazed to be offered a free sample of this nectar by a publicity van on Northcote Road. Disappointingly, Mum said we couldn't afford it and it wasn't good for me, and so Tizer remained the Sunday fizzy drink of choice in the Foster household. The yoyo was an instant success, and I should have loved to become a skilled practitioner of its dark arts. But I did not; I was doomed to be a failure, to be a grudging admirer of those girls and boys who could perform amazing feats of legerdemain with their new gadget. These tricks had fancy names like 'walk the dog', 'the creeper' and 'skin the cat'. I put my own lack of prowess down to my yoyo being a substandard model.

The diabolo also attempted a comeback and was briefly popular amongst the girls. My mum fished out her old model from her childhood and did a few tricks, but I think she had lost her touch. I dismissed it as rather old hat, and in any case its success was a flash-in-the-pan and lasted only a month or so.

---

[34] *I could bore for England on the subject of fivestones, but I am a humane man and will spare you the riveting details, dear reader.*

Skipping was permanently in vogue amongst the girls and they were extremely proficient. I was ambivalent towards skipping. On the one hand it was a girls' pastime and therefore cissy for a boy to be caught doing it. It also involved knowing a lot of soppy rhymes and chants off by heart, so that you could sing along to the beat of the skipping-rope. On the other hand, it required great nimbleness, balance and sure-footedness, like dribbling in football, as well as manual dexterity and stamina, and I knew that boxers skipped to build up their strength and fitness before a fight. Out of embarrassment, I usually avoided being involved in skipping, but sometimes it was impossible not be roped in, if you will excuse the pun, by enthusiastic nice girls or bossy girls. It was humiliating to be found wanting, to get my feet tangled up in the rope and mess up the game. I also found that the responsibility of swinging the rope round rhythmically and at the required speed weighed heavily and made me tense. Girls were great organisers of constructive play in the lane outside the school. There was more than one song and ritual dance that involved forming an arch, whilst the other children paraded through in pairs or single file, including 'London Bridge is falling down' and 'Oranges and Lemons', which ends with the charmingly gruesome 'here comes the chopper to chop off his head'.

Another of their favourite activities and one they never seemed to tire of, involved dancing round in a circle, with a boy or a girl in the middle, singing:

On the mountain stands a lady,
Who she is I do not know,
All she wants is gold and silver,
All she wants is a nice young man,
So come in my (Johnny) -oh
While I go out to play.
How many kisses will he give her?
One! Two! Three!

Although I always affected reluctance to join in, I confess that I quite liked being part of this game, as there was just an outside chance of one day being chosen. I secretly liked it when girls were flirtatious, even though I would of course have been mortified to be obliged to kiss one of them.

We children were allowed a good deal more freedom than 21st century children. I have already explained how, from the age of five, I was allowed to make what would now be considered a perilous half mile journey between home and school four times a day. From about seven years old onwards, I would disappear into the woods with a couple of pals for a whole afternoon, or on to the Docker to make touch-burners[35] or dig up liquorice-root to chew on, until our stomachs called us home for tea. The Docker was a colossal mound of shale and clay on the Cutting (Carrfield Road), grown over by rough grass and scrub, which provided a splendid area for children to have adventures away from annoying adult supervision.

It was completely normal for a small group of us lads to go on the 34 bus to Graves Park and play football or cricket, depending on the season. Autumn, winter and early spring, up until Cup Final day, were for football; summer was for cricket. There were no exceptions to this rule. It was almost as if football was forbidden in the summer months. Whatever the sport, we would play for hours on end, until we were exhausted, or hungry, or somebody was hurt and needed first-aid from his mum. In the weeks between Easter and Whitsuntide, it was forbidden to play games on the grass in the parks, and the park-keepers were very strict on this rule. There was one nice 'parky' who knew us well, winked, and took us to a hidden area of flat grass which was ideal for our games. We considered it our own pitch from then on and were narked if ever any other boys trespassed on it.

Because there were usually only three of us, Miffer (Ray Smith), Albert Wood and I, our football games were often not very adventurous, being confined to taking penalties and free kicks and being goalkeeper in turn. If Michael Howson came, we could have a two aside game, which was better, but he was a bit of a wimp and had a range of excuses not to come out with us. Occasionally we would bump into some other lads and play a proper game with them. Once a group

---

[35] *Touchburners were small, rectangular boxes made of clay, with holes in the four sides and no lid. We stuffed them with rags, set fire to the rags and ran along holding them high above our head, so that smoke puthered out behind us. They rarely worked well!*

of lads from Hollythorpe challenged us to a five-aside match the following day. We took up the gauntlet, in the name of Upper Heeley. I was ten, Albert and Miffer were a year older and in J4. Albert was keen enough, but he was pretty useless to be honest; Miffer was a bit better but very short, and only grew to about five foot three as an adult. Michael was not keen, and so I enlisted two of my cousins, Geoff, who was five, and Robert who was eight, or nearly eight. Robert was a good player, but Geoff was useless, and only five. My mum strapped her old hockey pads onto his legs, which made it very difficult for the poor lad to move, let alone run. However, it made him invulnerable to kicks on the shins, and he turned out to be a Trojan defender, though admittedly a little static, very brave, a great blocker of shots, and an accidental tripper-upper, getting under the feet of the opposition being his speciality. After the match, I reported back to his mum, Auntie Annie, that he had been a terrific member of the team, and I was proud of him. We lost the match, unsurprisingly, but were not disgraced.

While I'm on the subject of football in Graves Park, the leather case-ball story is worth relating. I had always craved a real 'casey', which is the name we gave to a real leather football with a bladder that you could blow up, like the ones used in professional matches, a so-called case-ball. My dream came true the Christmas before my tenth birthday. I was over the moon. No-one else that I knew had a casey. I would be the envy of all my pals. I was so happy, that I took my ball, size 4, match quality, off to show Miffer, who lived in Fitzroy Road, next to Memmott's shop. The ball had not yet been kicked, but I had dubbined all the stitching between the panels, and it was in pristine condition. A big lad grabbed the ball from me, saying 'let's have a look at thi casey, kid'. I grabbed it back, dropped it, and it bounced into the road in the path of a lorry and was crushed, with a loud bang. I was sick as a parrot.

I imagine my dad was fairly sick about the matter also, as a casey was an expensive item.

My birthday is on January 10th, and I must have appeared so heartbroken that my parents stumped up to buy me a second casey as my birthday present. Once more, I was over the moon. And very grateful, fully aware that I didn't really deserve it. The fate of the second casey was something of an improvement on the first, but equally final. For its first outing, I took the ball to Graves Park with the lads later in the month. We bumped into five other lads and had a game of four aside between us. We used their ball, which was okay by me, as mine would not get worn out or muddy. Instead, we used mine as one of the goalposts. Goalposts were, of course, usually coats or jumpers. We were playing 'goalie-wag-ness', so that there was not always one of us standing idle and shivering in goal. Goalie-wagness, a corruption of 'goalie when necessary', I suppose, meant that one player could be the designated goalkeeper, but could also play out and do the exciting stuff. The rule was used in small-sided games. Sometimes it was agreed that anybody could be goalie-wag-ness. Back to the fate of my casey. Whilst we were all down at one end of the pitch, furiously attacking or defending the far goal and giving this our full attention, one lad pointed out that one of our goalposts was missing. My casey! Someone had thieved it whilst we were all down at the other end of the pitch. Once again, I was sick as a parrot. My parents showed admirable composure, and my father did not take the strop down to me. If I had been him, I might have been tempted.

Whilst broadly still on the theme of the surprising amount of freedom afforded to young children, I should include an account of a little expedition to Doncaster, led by Albert Wood, almost 10, and yours truly, aged nine, and accompanied by cousin Geoffrey, aged four. The visit was occasioned by our temporary craze for spotting BRS numbers and checking them off in our BRS Spotters Handbook. Normal boys of the period were trainspotters and had the appropriate Train Spotters Handbook, but we considered ourselves a cut above, singled out from the herd, and therefore superior.

In case you are wondering what in heaven's name BRS was, it was short for British Road Services, the new nationalised road haulage system. Each lorry had a number, which indicated its origin, and every single lorry was listed in our handbooks. The true gems for the BRS spotter were the Scots, which had a special prefix. To spot BRS lorries, it was of course essential to take up a vigil on a trunk road. A major difficulty was that their identity numbers were on the cab door, and so sharp eyes were needed, first to identify the lorry as BRS and then to read the number as the lorry passed. Albert had received intelligence from a more experienced BRS spotter contact of his that the national trunk road, the A1, was the place to go for top spotting.

In 1949, the A1 ran directly through the centre of Doncaster. Having received appropriate parental permission and financial backing, we three musketeers each bought our own day return tickets from Sheffield Midland, ran from Doncaster station and took up our position on the steps of a war memorial in the centre of the A1 carriageway, having dashed across recklessly in a gap in the traffic. I realise now, of course, that BRS spotting was perhaps not the healthiest way for young lads to spend a summer's day, but I remember that Albert and I were very excited at the prospect of spotting Scots, and Albert's pal had tipped us off that this war memorial was the best place for Scots in the whole country, as it afforded close access to both north- and southbound traffic. We had taken provisions for lunch and were all set for a long vigil. What my cousin Geoffrey was doing along with us I have no idea. There cannot have been the slightest pleasure for him in sitting confined to the War Memorial steps, breathing in diesel fumes, bored out of his mind for a whole day, save of course for the thrill of being allowed out for the day with older boys.

I confess that at the end of the day I had found our expedition unrewarding. We were hot, dirty from the traffic grime, had headaches from breathing in the diesel fumes, and had only bagged three Scots the whole day. Secretly I had decided that the BRS game was not worth the candle and resolved to spend my time more profitably in future, playing cricket. I was relieved when Albert finally looked at his watch – he was the only one of us who had a watch – and declared reluctantly that it was time for tea and we would have to go home.

There was, when we arrived at Doncaster station, further disappointment. Cousin Geoffrey had irresponsibly lost his return train ticket. Each of us only had one penny left, enough for the bus fare home from Sheffield Midland. I upbraided Geoffrey severely, and he became sulky and unreasonably resentful towards me. I threatened to leave him in Doncaster, although I knew that this was a sanction I dared not impose for fear of parental retribution. I was supposed to be looking after him.

At this point the long arm of the law stepped in to resolve our problem. A local bobby enquired as to the reason for our collective dismay, and when I told him the sad tale, he gave Geoffrey a shilling to buy another ticket back to Sheffield. I was a little miffed that Geoffrey made a small profit on the deal and wasn't even going to suffer for his incompetence. I told him I was going to tell on him to his mum, and he would get a cop-it from her[36]. The ingrate then just sulked all the way back to Sheffield, standing in the corridor, and refused to come to sit with us in our compartment.

There was still time for one further twist to this tale. When we arrived at the ticket barrier in Sheffield, the feckless four-year-old once again had no ticket, however many times he rummaged in every pocket. I told the railway official the sad story of the lost ticket in Doncaster and of the merciful bobby, and he too took pity on us all and let my incompetent cousin through without a ticket. It turned out that Geoffrey had discovered what he thought was the original, lost ticket somewhere in a secret pocket and had thrown it out of the corridor window to avoid further righteous rage from me and an even more severe cop-it from his mum. However, the ticket that he threw out of the train window was not the original, lost ticket but the second ticket obtained through the good graces of the Doncaster bobby. I told him I would never ever take him anywhere ever again and sent him to catch the bus home on his own.

We had three different teachers during our time at the Annexe, Miss Bronks, Mrs Jones, and Mr Flower. Mrs Jones was my first teacher at the school, and I was lucky to have her. She was a woman of a certain age, experienced, kind but firm. You didn't mess with Mrs Jones, nor did you want to, as being in her class made you want to learn. I remember her as calm, smiling, and encouraging. And wearing a cardigan. In the afternoons she often read us stories such as Milly-Molly-Mandy, Uncle Remus, Just William, Rudyard Kipling's Just So stories, and Wandering with Nomad. Occasionally we even read a poem together. Liberal studies in-

---

[36] A 'cop-it' was a reprimand, or even a punishment.

deed! I loved the Uncle Remus stories, and of course my favourite character was Brer Rabbit, because he was so clever and always outwitted Brer Fox, or any other Brer whose turn it was to be humiliated. In later years, going back to the original in an attempt to rediscover childhood delights, I found the language difficult, the stories unappealing and Brer Rabbit far too much of a Clever Dick. Mrs Jones must have had a special storytelling talent.

Wandering with Nomad was not so riveting; these were stories in which the narrator, Nomad, instructed us about what there was to see in the countryside at various seasons of the year. I can't have learnt very much from the well-meaning Nomad, as I am a complete dunce when it comes to recognising flowers, trees and birds, but at least it was an opportunity for me to drift off into a world of my own and do a little recreational day-dreaming.

Milly-Molly-Mandy was engaging and entertaining enough, and I quite envied her living in a thatched cottage in a village, but she was a girl and a bit dull. I preferred the laddish adventures of the *Just William* stories. Even though his Home Counties world seemed light years from mine, and often he and his pals were just plain stupid, I would have loved to be one of his Outlaws. It was, however, a strange and confusing common feature of all these stories, that none of them bore the slightest relationship to real life as I experienced it. I could only surmise that our own lives were too insignificant to have stories written about us.

My second teacher at the Annexe, in J2, and a different classroom, was Mr Flower, whom I liked well enough and I was eager to please. He was younger than Mrs Jones, had short, dark brown hair and wore a tweed jacket. I have only two clear memories of interactions with Mr Flower. The first is that he was very keen on good behaviour, silence and paying attention. I guess, on reflection, that he was an inexperienced teacher and the insistence on silence may have been out of insecurity. We were not a disorderly lot, although there were 34 of us, and so there may have been a subdued hubbub in the room while we were doing our sums or learning our tables. This no doubt led to the incident when Mr Flower unaccountably lost his patience with us and told us he had had enough, the whole class had to do a hundred lines, to be handed in first thing in the morning. I remember feeling upset and personally responsible that we had somehow let him down, and I was keen to show him that I was on his side and wanted to be a good boy. After school dinner, instead of playing, I ran home and asked mum for some paper, explaining that I had to do a hundred lines. I sharpened a pencil and wrote 'For Mr Flower' and my own name at the top of the page. Then I used a ruler to draw a hundred very neat and precise straight lines across the paper, front and back. It was a work of art. My mum tried to explain that this was probably not what the teacher had meant, but I was determined to carry out the task scrupulously. I raced back to school and proudly handed in my imposition at afternoon register. Mr Flower seemed surprised, but accepted the paper without further comment. Perhaps he had realised the absurdity of giving a class of 8-year-olds a hundred lines, or my response to the punishment had helped him realise this, but the hundred lines were never mentioned again, and he never lost his patience with us for the rest of the year.

My second memory of Mr Flower was of his organising a football match against the Main School, in Graves Park on a Saturday morning. This was a memorable event because extra-curricular activities at the school simply did not exist in those times. It was memorable also as the first 11-a-side match that I played in. He announced his plan for the match and asked the class to decide upon a captain for the Annexe XI. My name was put forward and Mr Flower asked me to select a team of eleven lads, as I knew best who were the good players. I was well aware that we did not have a wealth of talent. Apart from John Jepson, who was pretty good, and Kenneth Lawson and George Knowles who were tough, there no automatic choices. On the other hand, there was no question of hurting anyone's feeling by leaving him out, as there were only about 17 lads in the class. Between us, Mr Flower and I arrived at a squad of 11 volunteers and pressed men, all reasonably able bodied. Girls were, of course, not considered for selection. That would have been outrageous. We all arrived on the 34 bus and met Mr Flower at the gates of Graves Park in time for a 10 o'clock kick-off, amazingly everyone turning up on time. The match itself, although played on a full-sized pitch with proper goalposts, was an undistinguished melee, whose quality disappointed me as a football purist. I had been expecting something which closer resembled the events that I usually witnessed at Bramall Lane of a Saturday afternoon. It turned out that the Main School team, despite having massive superiority of selection base, were no better than us, and it was not the David vs Goliath occasion that I was expecting. Somehow the ball was scrambled into each goal an equal number of times, and Mr Flower declared an honourable draw. I remember feeling quite proud.

It was a few months after Mr Flower's football match when the wider world rudely interrupted my cosy Heeley existence.

In the small world I was born into, Germans and Germany were our implacable enemy, dropped bombs on us, killed our brave Tommies. There was no room for argument; it was a fact. The Germans I knew from radio, comic books and films were ruthless, cruel, uniformed monsters who spoke in clichés: *Donnerwetter! Gott in Himmel! Achtung, Achtung! Schweinhund! Engländer 'raus!* Their language was consistently described as guttural, although I had only the vaguest idea what guttural meant – probably harsh or nasty in some way, I presumed.

Then, briefly but memorably, there came into my life a real German.

Karl stayed at my parents' invitation for two summer weeks as part of a group from eastern Germany. He was 13 or 14, blond, had no money and a colossal appetite, spoke rudimentary English, dressed in leather shorts and braces, and bowed his head and clicked his heels deferentially when addressing my parents.

I was relegated to the attic, but willingly gave up my bedroom for this fascinating stranger. I followed my mother like a shadow, as she showed him around our tiny house. I remember how she pointed to my bedroom: "Karl sleep here", he taking her to mean the narrow landing and saying "so small, Karl big". There were many moments of sheer comedy, a hundred hilarious misunderstandings. I remember the general hysterics when he would say Titty Hall instead of City Hall, his grumpy "too vide, too far" at having been obliged to walk home from the city centre, and my mother taking pity on him and giving him a precious twopence for bus-fare each day.

I remember also that he told us how pitifully poor his family were, how, as he swallowed his umpteenth slice of Gunstone's, how in Germany only invalids ate white bread. I remember the tears in his eyes, as he spoke of his father, gone to Russia, long time. I remember the tears from all three of us when he left. I never saw him again.

But I remember him.

And so it was that I chose to study German at grammar school and university, taught German, made a close, lifelong German friend and shared his passion for promoting international understanding. Germany was linked with my stars and became my second home.

Our teacher in J3 was Miss Bronks, a strict young woman with black spectacles and hair drawn severely back into a bun. I'm afraid I do not have any positive memories of Miss Bronks, whom I found unkind and often cruel. We were a well-behaved class – junior children did behave well at school in those days – and I don't remember there being any particularly difficult individuals. Admittedly we were a mixed bunch with a wide range of ability levels, and it may have been difficult to pitch lessons at the right level. I suspect anyway that there was precious little allowance made for children with learning difficulties, and there was no excuse for Miss Bronks's unwarranted severity, her constant ill-tempered moods and her frequent use of punishments. Her pet method of chastisement was to fetch the offending child out to the front of the class and rap him or her on the knuckles with a wooden ruler.

One particular morning sticks in my memory. First of all, to set the scene for the events of the morning, I should say that I was a very polite, well-behaved, hard-working little boy, a model pupil. On that morning I felt that Miss Bronks was being particularly unkind to Michael Storr, who we all knew found lessons difficult, but tried his best. I said 'that's not fair, shouting at Michael'. Miss Bronks called me to the front of the class and caned me on the hand for my rudeness. I was incensed by the injustice of it all. Vicki passed me a note saying 'that was not fair', shockingly rebellious behaviour for her. At morning playtime, I was still feeling peevish and decided I was not going to drink my milk. I poured it down a grate in protest at my unjust treatment. It was a kind of infant hunger strike, I suppose. One of the girls in the class snitched on me, and Miss Bronks caned me again as an example to the others. 'This is what we do to children who waste food. There are starving children in Africa.' I forget the precise reason for my third caning of the morning, but it was probably that I had become incensed with the injustice of it all and refused to do my work. Or perhaps I really was cheeky. I went home at dinner-time with very sore hands, and my mum kept me from school for the afternoon. She said she was going shopping, but I found out years later that she had gone into the school to speak to Mr Vaizey, the senior teacher, whom we called the Headmaster.

This was the only time I was ever caned at school, except for one occasion at secondary school, when Mr Kopcke dealt me three very painful strokes of the cane on my backside, while I was bent over gripping the banister of the upper corridor, this as retribution for drawing a picture on my desk - a footballer scoring a goal, if you're wondering. The Headmaster, Mr N.L. Clapton, called me to his study, fined me one shilling for this criminal damage to school property, and told me that there were far better ways for me to leave my mark on the school, a punishment which added insult to injury.

It was customary to have Mr Vaizey in J4. He was slim, older than the others, wore a dark suit and combed his short, brilliantined dark hair straight back, with a precise centre parting like my dad's. There was a protruding blue vein on his temple, which I found fascinating. I could not take my eyes off it. He was known to be very strict, and we all were in awe of his reputation. Nobody messed about in Mr Vaizey's class. If any boy was in trouble for misbehaviour (rare) or fecklessness (less rare) he was sent to Mr Vaizey for a feared reprimand. Equally, he was known to be fair, but even though I knew it was unlikely I would ever be sent for the Vaizey tongue-lashing, I kept my distance when he was around.

To my delight, we found we were not to have Mr Vaizey in J4, but my favourite teacher, Mrs Jones, once more. J4 was the year of the feared Scholarship exams, as we called the eleven plus. In the autumn term our parents filled out a form on which they listed six grammar schools in order of preference. The top grammar schools, in order of preference, for boys on my side of the city, were generally acknowledged as King Edward's, High Storrs, Nether Edge, City Grammar, whereas in the northern part of the city Firth Park had high standing also. For girls, the top choices were High Storrs, Abbeydale Grange and Hurlfield, but there were a few scholarships available for high achievers at the fee-paying Sheffield Girls High School. These were all single-sex schools. In their wake trailed schools that we thought of as semi-grammar schools, like Central Tech and the brand new Rowlinson School, which was mixed. This may not have been how the Education Authority intended the system to be, but it was certainly how we perceived it. There were also Catholic Grammar Schools available, Notre Dame for girls and De la Salle for boys, but as we had no Catholics at the Annexe, these did not come under consideration. If you didn't 'pass' the Scholarship exam, in other words didn't rank high enough to attain one of your choices, you were assigned to the 'secondary modern' school nearest to you, usually mixed.

The three tests, arithmetic, English and a third, puzzle-solving IQ type of test were nervously anticipated by all. Even I, who loved doing tests and puzzles, was apprehensive, as we had been made fully aware that our whole future hung on the outcome. We sat the tests in the late spring and received the letter informing us of the school we had been assigned to at the end of the summer term. Michael Gould and I were to be sent to King Edward's, his brother Robert and the two Davids to High Storrs, Pat Earnshaw to Rowlinson, Vicki to the Girls High and the rest of the class mostly to the local secondary modern school. It was expected, but nevertheless it was a severe parting of the ways, a turning point in our lives, perhaps especially so for me.

VIII School days: King Ted's

I now entered my fish-out-of-water period. In the summer holiday before I started at KES, my mother and I went to t' Stores to buy my new school uniform, which consisted of navy blue blazer, blazer badge, grey short trousers, grey school socks, grey school jumper, school tie, school cap and badge, school scarf, black formal shoes, leather satchel, gym shoes, football boots, gym shorts and vest, house team shirt and socks, woodwork apron, special swimming trunks and cap, embroidered labels for my clothes, maths and geometry sets, fountain pen, and various other prescribed stationery items for my new life amongst the clever boys at the city's elite centre of learning.

I am not sure how my parents managed to pay for all this. I was eleven and it did not occur to me at the time to ask myself the question. It was only in the later years at the school that I began to realise the extent of their financial sacrifice. In the fifth and sixth form, for instance, I told my mum I no longer needed to wear a uniform blazer and wore instead a shabby old sports jacket, with leather patches sewn onto the elbows. This was frowned upon by the establishment. It was made clear to me that this was unacceptable clothing, I would be regarded as not sound, and I could therefore never be chosen as a school prefect. Perhaps this accentuated the feeling I had always had of not quite belonging. I ploughed my own furrow and thrived well enough in the sixth form, carrying off several of the school's prizes and raising some eyebrows by winning a State Scholarship, justification enough perhaps for a few minor deviations from conformity.

Parents and the general public were not encouraged inside most secondary schools at those times. There were no parents' evenings, no open days. Nor did I personally set foot inside the school until the first day of term in September 1951. There was nothing so revolutionary as an induction day for new boys. At King Edward's, apart from school concerts and plays, tickets for which sold like hot cakes, parents did not enter the building. Until, in my final year at the school, out of the blue an Open Evening was announced, like a snap election. In the preceding days, there was much fluttering in the dovecotes, as teachers prepared displays for their classrooms. The magazine photograph of Betty Gable, captioned *Betty Gables Beine*[37], whose presence for several years had always puzzled me, as I considered it rather risqué for King Ted's, disappeared from the wall of the German room. Nothing much happened at this open evening. Parents meandered around the corridors glancing into the classrooms and venturing into rooms of special interest, like their son's geography room, the swish new library, or the chemistry lab. *Glasnost* it was not, but I suppose it was a start. As to my parents, my dad wore a suit, a white shirt, and a tie and looked, I thought, rather like the late George VI. My mum, giving a passable impression of the Queen Mother, held a short conversation with Mr Oppenheimer, my German teacher, and my dad listened.

I was assigned on my first day to class 1(2), with Mr Hemming as my form tutor. As we 30 boys queued in a long snake outside the classroom waiting to enter, the tiny, bespectacled boy behind me, who I later learned was Georgie Smith, from Attercliffe, a working-class, industrial sector of the city, gave me an unsolicited piece of advice: 'tha's got to gerrin wi t' teachers'.[38] We English identify each other's social class within the first ten seconds of meeting, by our accents. I spotted Georgie Smith as even more out of his depth than I was. At least I could manage a fair approximation of the Queen's English. I didn't doubt the wisdom of his advice, although I was unsure of its morality and was even less certain that Georgie would be able to ingratiate himself

---

[37] *Betty Gable's legs*
[38] *You have to ingratiate yourself with the teachers.*

with the posh teachers. Our paths diverged after the first year at the school, and so I am not sure if he achieved his goal. I doubt it.

Mum and Dad in their Sunday best

As I had expected, life was very different from at the Annexe. First of all, I would never during my seven long years at the school, not even once, be called John by any master, nor by any boy. The masters addressed me as Foster, the classmates called me Foz. More formally, I was JS Foster, or occasionally Foster JS. Equally surprisingly, the masters were often referred to simply by their initials. There were no women teachers, presumably because there were none good enough to nurture our thoroughbred male brains. One element of the establishment that was comfortingly familiar was the similarity with life at the fictional Red Circle School, featured in dozens of the stories I had read and loved in the *Hotspur*. For instance, I recognised the House system, the Forms[39], the uniform, the lofty and obviously noble Head Boy and his smart sixth form prefects, the Latin school motto[40]. All the boys were clever, some of them cleverer than me, it turned out, which was something of a shock to the system. French, Latin and science were all new to me, as were woodwork and art lessons, PE in the gym, and games afternoons.

I loved the games afternoons, but there was a snag. Because I was sure that all the King Edward's boys would be swots, geeky, weedy and wear glasses, I expected to be the best footballer and to lord it over the others. Instead, in the hurly-burly of the massed ranks of the 240 small boys in the first and second forms I was cast aside and relegated to play with the 'Pickups'. My first rejection at the school. The 'Pickups' were the rest of the boys after the house teams had been picked. There were eight houses, each with 30 boys in the Lower School, and only 11 could be chosen to be whisked off on buses to Castle Dyke for the league matches. The rest were consigned to a free-for-all on the two pitches at Whiteley Woods, and so, if we discount the sick and the lame, the matches were about 20 a side. In this company I was indeed able to lord it, if ever the ball happened to come my way.

My house was Lynwood, the only house not to be named after a country estate[41], but whose name was a legacy of a former boarders' house[42]. I spent three Tuesday afternoons in the purgatory of the 'Pickups' before my goalscoring prowess reached the ears of house-captain Rutledge and I was selected as centre forward in the Lynwood XI posted on the House noticeboard. The match was against Clumber,

---

[39] *Although disappointingly there was no Form called the Remove, and I had always wanted to know what that was!*

[40] fac recte nil time – *act honourably, fear nothing*

[41] *The other houses were Arundel, Chatsworth, Clumber, Haddon, Sherwood, Welbeck and Wentworth.*

[42] *Firstly, in the Headmaster's own house in Collegiate Crescent, later in Clarkehouse Road.*

who wore maroon jerseys. I wore my voluminous[43] blue and white quartered team shirt with pride. Lynwood had by now already lost the first three matches, and were expected to lose again, but we won 5-2, and I still recall the warm glow of my first real experience of being part of a team, the joy of winning together. Rutledge especially made me feel at home, for the first time at the school, and I am grateful to him. If I ever had a sense of belonging at King Edward's it was through Lynwood House. Our housemaster was Mr Twyford, a hefty, lumbering chap, whose classroom was in an attic, up a narrow flight of stairs. He was my teacher for French and for maths in my first year at the school, and so I spent a great deal of time in this attic room, assigned to the same seat throughout, in the back corner, as far as it was possible to be from the teacher. I sat next to a boy called Jon Buchan, whose father was an English master and should have known better! Buchan, a quiet lad and a decent cove, was a pretty lousy footballer, but tackled like a professional and later became school football captain.

Back to Mr Twyford. His desk was on a raised dais in the far corner of the room from me, and I can say with complete honesty that never once in the whole year of maths and French lessons did he rise from his seat. Admittedly, there was little room for him to parade around between the rows to inspect our work and progress, especially so considering his massive bulk, but I suspect that even in the most spacious of classrooms he would have remained stolidly seated. This is not to say that I have any complaint about Mr Twyford, who gave me a sound enough basis of knowledge in these two subjects. He was a warm-hearted, ruddy-faced, middle-aged, corpulent stereotype, but the warmheartedness was welcome. And we had Lynwood in common. In my last two years at the school, when I had succeeded the great Rutledge in the soccer captaincy and we were in pursuit of the coveted senior house football trophy, Mr Twyford would watch our matches from the halfway line, swaddled in a huge greatcoat and scarf, reclining in his striped deckchair, pipe fired up, bellowing non-stop 'LYNWOOD! LYNWOOD!'. I

---

[43] *Mum wanted it to last a few years! I still have the shirt. It fits perfectly.*

loved him for that, and there have been very few prouder moments in my life than receiving the prestigious, gleaming silver football trophy from the Headmaster, in my shabby tweed jacket with patched elbows, in front of the whole school, and more importantly in front of Mr Twyford.

As well as being our form tutor, Mr Hemming taught my form English in our first year. He was obviously a nice man and did an excellent job of shepherding us through the early days. I always felt protected in his classroom. I remember the names of many of the other teachers in that first year: Messrs Barnes, Surguy, Helliwell and Watling spring to mind. Mr Barnes, our music teacher, was histrionic and seemed slightly mad. He encouraged us to sing vigorously for half an hour once a week during my one and only year of music lessons at the school. *Drake was in his cabin, Röslein rot, The drunken sailor,* and *Greensleeves* appeared to be particular favourites of his. Whilst most of the songs were posher than I was used to in my family's Sunday evening singalongs, I found the singing classes pleasant enough. Mr Barnes, though patently insane, brimmed with enthusiasm and encouraged even me to join the school choir as a member of the 'Troubles'. Much to my parents' delight, I appeared in both *the Messiah* and *Judas Maccabeus* at a packed Victoria Hall, where their seats were, purely by chance, in the centre of the balcony and made them 'feel like royalty'. Mr Barnes was the revered Director of Music at the school for three decades and famously wrote the revised version of the music for the school song, which was in Latin, and was sung every morning in the Assembly. I still know it by heart.

Mr Surguy was never entirely satisfied at my efforts with the saw, the hammer, the chisel, and more especially the plane. My woodwork classes had all the characteristics of a recurring nightmare. I presented him with yet another painstaking but pathetic effort at planing a piece of softwood. He slid his metal set-square across my planed surfaces, saying 'here, here and here', and marked my deficiencies with his pencil. Ad infinitum. And nauseam too, for that matter. Against the odds, I improved a little in woodwork in the second year and once made, in my opinion if not his, an almost passable mortise and tenon joint, a model boat that floated, admittedly on its side, and a much-appreciated plywood pipe-rack for my uncle Ron. Nevertheless, the comments that Mr Surguy made on my school report did not encourage me to become a professional carpenter.

My one and only year of art, with Mr Helliwell, is best passed over quickly without too much comment. I found him disagreeable in the extreme. I remember him as a short, scruffy man with a bushy moustache, who wore a scruffy smock and smelt of tobacco. Clarence, as he was known to us boys, was not at all interested in my work, never spoke to me let alone give me any advice, never even looked me in the eye. In our end of year examination, we were instructed to draw a frieze. I had a vague idea what a frieze was – our front room wallpaper had one, I believed - but no real clue as to what was actually wanted by Mr Helliwell. I did my level best and drew some neat patterns round the edge of an A4 sheet of paper. Mr Helliwell awarded me 7%, possibly for writing my name on the paper. I believe this may be a school record. I was destroyed. The credit for my artistic skills goes entirely to you, Clarence. You taught me, or rather didn't teach me.

Mr Twyford

Clarence Helliwell

Mr Harrison was my teacher for PE and for swimming in the first form. I enjoyed his lessons well enough and found him an agreeable enough teacher who was relaxed and didn't shout at us. Harrison had that natural authority that I have seen in practically every PE teacher I have come across. It apparently goes along with the role and even seems to carry over to their second-string subject in the classroom. As these were single lessons and our lessons were only 35 or 40 minutes long, this was an early education in the knack of getting undressed, then showered, dried and dressed again quickly and efficiently, a skill which in later life some boys no doubt found useful for clandestine affairs, or more innocently to avoid being late for work.

Disappointingly, both geography and history turned out to be subjects as arid as the Atacama desert. V.J. Wrigley was my history teacher and left me cold in lesson after lesson. He killed any interest I might have had with consummate expertise. I remember just one moment of significant interest in history lessons during the whole year. One morning, a small boy was sent round the school with a message that King George had died. Wrigley read out the message, paused for a few seconds, dismissed the boy and carried on lecturing.

Geography was with Mr Kopcke, and the year did have one enjoyable highlight. For half a term in the summer, we were given the task of researching Australia. Our results were to be presented as a foolscap-sized map filled with information, in the form of symbols and notes, that we had gleaned from our textbook. I enjoyed this a good deal and gave it my full attention, much of the time with my tongue slightly out, so as to concentrate better. I dare say Mr Kopcke enjoyed it too, as he will have had a relaxing half term. At any rate, he was more than usually complimentary about my finished product, which I was allowed to take home to show my parents. I now felt I was quite the expert on Australia. Perhaps Mr Kopcke was generous in grading my work because I had previously been a geography dunce. One of the funniest teacher stories I have heard was told to me by a geography colleague at Westfield School in Sheffield. He had spent half a term studying the pampas with the aptly named 3Z. They had watched films, listened to schools radio broadcasts, drawn maps and graphs, and generally 'done' the pampas right royally. He was now dutifully checking pupils' progress. He asked one boy to tell him what he knew about the pampas. Silence. Could he, for instance, show him where it was on the map? Silence. Perhaps he could tell him in his own words where the pampas was? The boy nodded confidently, drew a deep breath and said 'Well, tha knows Eckington Church . . .'

In the second form, my geography teacher was Mr Towers, Bert Towers to us. Bert was a notorious user of the epidiascope, a kind of forerunner to the overhead projector, and the only example in the school. By some kind of sorcery, I presume via a series of lenses, mirrors and prisms, Bert could project the image of the page of a book onto a screen at the front of the class. As use of a bright overhead light in the mechanism was necessary to the procedure, many of his lessons were conducted in a penumbral gloom, with windows shut and blinds drawn, creating a soporific effect. I have often since wondered what happened to the epidiascope and why it did not find further utility in the classrooms of the world. At any rate, I found Mr Towers no more engaging than his predecessor, and when forced to choose between geography and history, at the end of the second form, I made the somewhat surprising choice of history.

This turned out to be probably the worst choice I ever made at the school. My teacher was to be JBA Burridge, whom I found contemptuous, arrogant and remote. Our curriculum was the politics of 18th and 19th century England, presumably his specialist period. Walpole and Pitt featured strongly, if in my case, not memorably. In my recollection, Burridge was a snob and a bully, and I hated his lessons. He had favourites and was so universally disliked that it was rumoured around the sixth form that he had dubious relationships with older boys, a rumour that I dismissed as tittle-tattle. Although I paid attention in class, I never for one moment felt included. I worked hard at my revision before the O level examination, but on the day my mind was a blank, and I realised I had understood nothing. The only advice from Burridge to the class that I remember is that you could get a decent bottle of claret for seven and sixpence, I forget where, as it was information totally useless to me; claret was alien to my domestic circumstances. The history question paper covered the period from antiquity to the 20th century, and I ended up writing answers on Winston Churchill, Julius Caesar and Boadicea, because I had heard of them. It goes without saying that I failed English history O level.

In the fifth form, those boys in 5MS1[44] who were studying a foreign language at A level – and there was quite a bunch of us – were assigned to the young 'Daddy' Collins for a one-year crash course in 'modern' European history. Collins, who was strictly speaking an economics teacher, appeared inexperienced and often found it tricky to keep a large class of cocky 15 and 16-year-olds on track. He was the subject of many a practical joke. However, he retained his good humour throughout the school year, we were fond of him, and his lessons were interesting and engaging. He provided us with an excellent base of knowledge and understanding as a background to our studies of European litera-

---

[44] *MS was short for modern studies, the arts as opposed to the sciences.*

ture, a major part of the A level languages syllabus in the 1950s. We all passed the examination, and I personally felt that I had waltzed through the questions not only with confidence but also with enjoyment.

Maths was more my cup of tea. After all, it was merely an extension of 'Mental', which I loved. There were also fascinating adventures into areas called algebra and geometry, which required the use of an enigmatic codebook with sections called log tables, sines, cosines and tangents. These new fields of study engaged my interest immediately. My teachers following on from Mr Twyford were the affable Mr Ingham, who ran a football team and was therefore okay, Mr Burkinshaw, also a football coach, whom I found a sympathetic and expert teacher, and finally, in the fourth form, Mr Hersee, who was brisk and efficient and seemed to take a dislike to me for reasons I could not ascertain. Perhaps it was my imagination, but I found him brusque and unapproachable. Perhaps it was because I sat in the centre of the front row that he was constantly staring over my head and past me at other, worthier boys. In the mock O level exam in January, I performed well, scoring 97% and only 1% behind McLeod, the acclaimed mathematical genius of form 4(1) and the go-to pupil for answering tricky questions in class. Mr Hersee handed back my examination paper and pointed at me accusingly: 'you've been revising'. If it was congratulations, it certainly did not feel like it. It felt as though he were accusing me of unfair practice, or at the very least of slacking previously. For about two months before the actual O level examinations, we studied for a further examination called Additional Mathematics. This was much less of a walk in the park, encompassing as it did thorny areas like mechanics, integration, and differentiation. I passed the examination, but felt discouraged enough by the level of difficulty to dismiss any possibility of switching to A Level maths. Nor did Mr Hersee invite me into the magic inner circle of talented mathematicians urged to join the course. Q.E.D., I decided, stick to conjugating and declining, Foz.

The distinguished classicist, EF Watling, was the principal translator for Penguin Classics and was responsible for translating Sophocles's three Theban plays, nine plays by Plautus and the tragedies of Seneca. He also compiled regular crossword puzzles for *The Listener,* under the pseudonym Marcus, his nickname at the school. He was my teacher for three of my four years of Latin before 'O' levels. In my first year at the school, he was also my teacher for Scripture. His method of teaching Scripture was to set us 11-year-olds the task of reading an Old Testament story and drawing coloured pictures of it in our exercise books. He said very little to us except to urge us to be silent. Generally, we were. Little boys like to draw pictures and colour them in. That I learned any Latin at all at the school was in no way due to the efforts of EF Watling. He was very tall, stone deaf and totally incapable of keeping order. I was sorry for him at the time. I now realise that he showed zero interest in teaching, except perhaps when I was in the fifth form and a large group of us post O level students were assigned to him for an enlightening course in general classical literature, including the histories of Herodotus and the letters of Erasmus in the original Latin. Many of the boys in this group, who by now knew him by reputation, mocked him mercilessly and were very badly and at times lewdly behaved, leading to his flying into fearful rages of frustration. I was ashamed of my classmates at these times, as for once I knew that Marcus was doing his best and they were treading on something that he loved. Perhaps his disability had led to this state of affairs, led to him giving up on teaching. Or perhaps it was just laziness on his part, accepting a salary for nothing. At any rate, his method of teaching Lower and Middle School boys was to set us a task, to switch off his hearing aid so that he could hear nothing, and then sit at the front of the class, buried in his own thoughts. He was, by the time I left the school, 59 years old, with grey, thinning hair and grey skin. He retired two years later, after 36 years at King Edward's.

So, how did I learn any Latin? I hear you ask, anxious for my educational welfare. It happened like this. One Friday, the week before the annual examination at the end of my first year, with Marcus absent ill, one of the other Latin teachers, whose name escapes me, swept into our classroom and demanded that we demonstrate our knowledge of the imperfect tense. Most of us were baffled at the request. I personally had acquired a working knowledge of the perfect tense of the first conjugation and so, when he confronted me directly as a representative of the class's learning, I ventured a speculative 'amavi, amavisti, amavit' and was cut short by an exasperated snort from our visitor. He packed us off home with the brief of learning by heart the present, imperfect, perfect, pluperfect, future, and future perfect of the first three conjugations, over the weekend. I did as he had asked. The young brain is a miraculous soaker up of new knowledge, useful or not. In the second form, when I was in form 2A along with lots of swots like Miller and Fairest, whose fathers were university professors, we had 'Tug' Wilson for Latin. Tug had a reputation for fierceness, and, of all the teachers in the school, boys seem to be most in awe of him. He had what was reputed to be a war wound which had left him with a crippled or amputated arm. I said very little during that year, but I learnt a lot of Latin. By the third form, when I was in Form 3(1) and back with Marcus, I had 'learnt how to do it', I had my textbooks, and I got on with it.

My experience with Marcus was perhaps a microcosm of the learning experience at King Edward's. From the moment I walked into the building it was impossible not to imbibe the reverence for learning that it exuded; there were the gowned teachers, the solemn morning assemblies with the Latin school song, the imposing display boards in the hallway heralding in gold letters the achievements of its alumni. We were expected to behave like academics, and mostly we did. The quality of most of the teaching was woeful by today's standards and reflected the kind of teaching that the Masters had themselves received at public school, grammar school and university. They stood at the front of the class and filled us with facts. Mr Gradgrind and Mr McChoakumchild eat your hearts out. For me, they were remote, superior beings, on a different plane of existence and certainly members of a different social class. Before the sixth form, I can remember very few of them speaking to me personally, looking me in the eye, taking interest in my work, except to correct it with red ink. The science teachers I found particularly remote in the third and fourth forms. Our physics teacher was Mr Redston, Trotsky to us, probably because of his appearance and, as I discovered later, the fact that he had Russian parents. He was a fierce little man with short, curly hair and small, round spectacles, scowling, apparently angry, fearsome at any rate, and stood on a raised platform in the centre of the room and dictated knowledge to us, occasionally demonstrating physics phenomena for our edification. You could hear a pin drop from the moment we entered the physics lab, and not because we were in rapt fascination for the subject matter. I hated and feared those lessons, and he helped to destroy any ambition I might have had of being a scientist or a doctor, a profession I would love to have pursued. Our chemistry teacher, Mr Mackay, was almost equally fierce and remote, but at least we were allowed to conduct our own experiments in the laboratory. Mr Wastnedge was the exception. He taught us biology in forms 3(1) and 4(1) and was a kind, open, good-humoured, patient man. I remember one incident clearly with great affection. He was teaching us about fungus, how it grew on food and extended its cunning tendrils. I felt so at ease in his classroom that I even raised my hand and ventured a comment, most unusually for me, as can be seen from a brief perusal of my school reports, which all too frequently bemoan my reticence, my lack of confidence and my minimal contribution in class.

'Sir, sometimes a fungus grows on the top of my mum's jam.'

'Interesting.' He turned and smiled at me. 'And what does she do with it?'

'She scrapes it off and we eat the rest, sir.'

'And what you think she should do with it?'

'I think she should throw it away, sir.'

'That's correct. Well done, Foster (He knew my name!). You'd better tell her.'

I did. Triumphantly. And every biology lesson afterwards I could hardly wait to get to Mr Wastnedge's classroom. It doesn't take much to encourage a child to learn. That I remember this conversation even now, 67 years later, with such clarity, is highly significant. I guess I was always looking for a sympathetic teacher, a human being behind the academic gown.

One more science-related incident is perhaps worth recounting. Word got around, via the boys of $2a$, that the second form were 'doing' mercury, which was reported as great fun to play with, because of its comical tendency to run along like a silver ball-bearing, then to break up into lots of small balls in a highly entertaining fashion. Some of the boys in $2a$ had liberated samples of the mercury demonstrated in their lesson, and we 2A lads were agog at their tricks. Came our science lesson, we were, as hoped, each handed our small ration of the fascinating liquid metal, so that we could observe its characteristics studiously and note them down in our exercise book. We did, of course. Quite a number of us decided it would be amusing (and educational, of course) to continue our observations at home. I secreted my mercury in my handkerchief and tied a knot to prevent it from escaping. That afternoon, the drastic depletion in the school's stocks of mercury having been detected, science teachers were dispatched to all second form classes to interrogate suspects. It appeared principally to be a matter of theft rather than danger to our health, but the poisonous properties of mercury were definitely mentioned. Most boys cracked up under withering face-to-face questioning and handed in their stash of the deadly metal, but I held firm under interrogation and denied all involvement. I decided that telling a little white lie, as I thought of it, was a sin preferable to confessing to the serious crime of theft from the school. I had already learned that dishonesty was preferable to disgrace. Nevertheless, the mercury affair was a significant life-lesson, and the fear of discovery and its consequent shame and ignominy was sufficient to deter me from descending into a life of felony. In my post-mercury period, I became a model of probity. As to suffering from mercury poisoning, which might well have been appropriate karma, the evidence is only circumstantial, but I have thankfully no recollection of any symptoms of peripheral neuropathy or inhibition of my selenium-dependent enzymes. The question remains, what in heaven's name were the science teachers doing letting us handle mercury? Even in 1952. I may consider suing.

Our scientific education at the school in forms 1 to 4 was paltry, sketchy, inadequate. In forms 3 and 4 we had one hour each of chemistry, biology and physics. Three quarters of the boys in the fourth form sat the O level examinations a year early, typically in eight or nine subjects. For science we sat an examination called General Science, whose curriculum inevitably covered a minimal amount of ground in such a short time. After the Fourth Form, it was goodbye to science. We had done with it. Those boys who wanted a more thorough scientific education went on to study a fixed combination of chemistry, physics and maths, for two years to A level. This was felt to be the best preparation for further scientific and medical study at university. There appeared to be no other choice. If biology interested you, this interest was generally pursued as part of another combination of subjects, for instance geography. Biology was always considered a girls' subject and therefore inferior.

For those few boys who opted or, more accurately speaking, were selected for the Classical sixth form, the regime was brutal, with the A level course in Latin, classical Greek and ancient history completed in one school year, strictly speaking little over two terms. These stars were then expected to compete for scholarships and places at Oxbridge from the age of sixteen. Many were successful, *mirabile dictu*. As for myself, the choice was obvious. You did what you were good at, and my strength was modern languages. It was obvious that I should choose French and German, and their companion was usually considered to be English literature. I was keen to study economics, to add another string to my bow, but the timetable and the options system did not permit this maverick combination. Though I was no star in English classes, I was fond of Gerry Claypole, the Senior English master, whose love for his subject was patently sincere. Gerry was to become my form teacher for three years in the fifth and sixth forms. I remember him as cultured and scholarly, well-groomed and neatly dressed, in either corduroy or a linen jacket, gently smiling, polite to everyone, including me. No stickler for formalities, he kept a loose rein on his form members, occasionally not appearing for afternoon registration, which he trusted us to complete ourselves. His attitude to his English A level students was similar, periods of rather plain fare, unexceptional routine lessons, interspersed with bursts of enthusiasm and brilliant histrionic performances, when he would literally bound into the classroom and metaphorically grasp us by our intellectual throats.

As I have previously mentioned, my encounter with Rolf at an early age had awakened my interest in the German language and people. When presented with the choice of Spanish, classical Greek and German, it was a foregone conclusion which language I would opt for. The study of languages at King Edward's, as at most schools, was an academic affair, a series of knotty grammatical problems to be solved, the learning of lists of 'vocab', verb conjugations and tenses, declensions of nouns and adjectives, genders, and 'cases'. Latin had the nominative, accusative, genitive, dative and ablative, but German was missing the ablative case, and at first I found this a mystifying failure to conform. It was also written in an exotic script called 'Gothic', hard to decipher and an added element of code-breaking, which appealed to me. Furthermore, all its nouns without exception were awarded a capital letter! We practised saying German sentences, but at no time was there any real communication delivered in the foreign language, apart from perhaps 'Guten Tag'. Any important message, like 'come here, boy' or what was to be set for homework was conveyed in a language we could understand. This oral aspect was evidently considered essentially superfluous, no more than mere garnish[45]. I found that I was quite good at this new game and prospered especially in German classes, where there were fewer of us than for French.

My first teacher for German was Mr Kopcke, principally a geography teacher, but also a German speaker. I understand that he was later promoted to a post of Senior Geography Master in Germany. Subsequently, however, my main German teacher was JO, Mr JO Oppenheimer. Oppenheimer was a dispassionate professional, unruffled at all times, conscientious, strictly academic in his approach to teaching. He followed our progress closely, corrected and graded our work meticulously, and we learned well with him. Later, in the fifth and sixth form, although there were only four or five of us in his German class, I am sadly unable to claim that there existed a personal relationship with my teacher. Nor was there a real sense of group identity. This is not to say that JO was unfriendly, nor was he unkind. A question of chemistry, perhaps.

The Senior Modern Languages Master was EV 'Spiv' Bramhall. Spiv was a short, slim, dapper man, with a neatly

---

[45] *I attach no particular blame here to KES language teachers. This was how it was done at the time. My experience at University reflected exactly the same pattern. Absurdly, lectures and tutorials were all delivered in English.*

groomed pencil moustache and short, black hair, and often sported a bow-tie. A velvet smoking jacket comes to mind when I think of him, and even if he never wore one in his life, it is an image which conveys him perfectly. I remember him as bustling round the school in a businesslike manner, smiling benignly and looking important. His teaching technique was animated and histrionic, and indeed he could be a stimulating and amusing master. He had style. Boys seemed to be fond of him, in a 'good-old-Spiv' way, but although he was my French teacher for a number of years, I never fathomed out whether he was genuine or whether the external appearance of professionalism and bonhomie concealed feet of clay. He was not from any world that I recognised, and I found him unapproachable. *Mea culpa*, perhaps, but in all the years he taught me, I felt that he never went so far as to acknowledge my presence in the classroom, and his school reports on my French revealed that he hardly knew who I was, even in the sixth form. I have a bone to pick with Spiv, too, about my final year at the school. After our first shot at A levels, in the Lower Sixth, we stayed on for a further year to prepare for the Oxbridge entrance examinations and to sit what was known as the S level, or sometimes AS level. Along with sitting the A level exams a second time, we also sat two extension papers in our specialist subjects, in my case French and German language and literature. My French group was timetabled for a double lesson on Thursday mornings with Spiv, for coaching and extra study. He graced us with his presence for the first session and indulged us with his special charm, we turned up faithfully every Thursday morning in the hope of hearing wise words on Racine or Baudelaire, but Spiv only appeared on two more occasions, once very briefly at that, during the whole year. We didn't complain. I am complaining now, Spiv. I hope you're listening.

One other languages teacher played a major role in my education at King Edward's, and of all the teachers I met he is the one dearest to my heart. Olaf Raymond Johnston, ORJ, taught the French A level class and also shared the German A level teaching with JO. Consequently, we saw a great deal of each other in the classroom. I first met ORJ in the second form, when he was my French teacher. He was in his second post, full of energy, loved to have fun and make jokes in the classroom, and we small boys simply loved him. Admittedly there was a certain amount of chaos in his room, but between the laughs we learned well enough. One day, we watched him, intrigued, as he cleared the teacher's desk and then built a small staircase of books. He produced a box from his briefcase, then from the box what appeared to be a steel spring, which he stretched like an accordion, affecting an air of a magician. He placed it on the top step of his construction and set it off on a series of somersaults down the stairway. We were on our feet, applauding and caterwauling with glee! It was, of course, our first sight of the famous slinky, a toy which delighted so many children for decades. He had come across it at a toy fair. Shortly afterwards, I spent a week in the Royal Hospital undergoing surgery on my sinuses. As a boy, I had always suffered badly with coughs and colds, and the doctors had decided to try to cure me. I spent a further week at home, recuperating. During this week, one of my class, Michael Gould, who of course knew where I lived, delivered a package to me from ORJ and the French class. It was a slinky. I regard this as a measure of the man. I certainly received no other gesture so personal or so generous from any other master.

In the sixth form classes, with his small group of admirers, ORJ was able to give free rein to his personality. As we already knew, he loved fun, and we discovered he was a big fan of The Goons, of humour in the style of Sellar and Yeatman's *1066 and All That*, and of shaggy dog stories – he told us at least one every week without fail, and we prided ourselves in seeking out one to tell him in return. When he knew I needed a German dictionary for my University course, he offered me the one he had used at University, in Gothic script, naturally. His name and college are inscribed on the fly-leaf, in immaculate handwriting. It is outdated and now sits unused on my bookshelves, but I treasure it still.

One staggering incident during my upper sixth year revealed to me that not all the members of staff were po-faced academics after all. There were a few others, it transpired, who shared ORJ's sense of humour. Completely unannounced, so that only a few sixth formers got wind of it that very morning of the event, a small group of teachers, apparently led by Mr Arthur (alias BCA) and the genial and popular TK Robinson, an economics master, staged a sort of *Beyond the Fringe* cabaret show in the lecture theatre, a benevolently satirical commentary on school life. The lucky boys who witnessed the spectacle, including my bosom pals Bro, Rad and Ogg, were in seventh heaven. We could hardly believe our own eyes. Mr Arthur ran a football team, and I already found him sympathetic enough, even though I had never been in his class for French or Latin. That lunchtime he became a hero. He announced the show by beating dramatically on a gong, whilst a colleague held up a placard saying A RANK ARTHUR PRODUCTION, a parody which immediately launched us into paroxysms of laughter from which we did not recover, as the teachers hammed their way through a corny script for the next half hour. It was amateurish, but hilarious. We few, we happy few, we band of brothers, made the lecture theatre echo with our applause. Whether or not the affair came to the ears of our unsmiling headmaster, NL Clapton, nor what he thought of such frivolity if it did, we shall never know. Perhaps he too was a bundle of laughs in private. Somehow I think not.

Only once did ORJ's good humour fail him. Only once did I find him pompous. The musical *My Fair Lady* was in vogue, and one of the lads came into the classroom singing 'With a little bit of luck'. ORJ became angry and told us that this song was symptomatic of all that was wrong in our something-for-nothing society. I was shocked at his reaction and wanted to tell him that he was wrong, it was all just a joke, and none of us took the song seriously, but it was clearly not the moment, and I was a boy and he was a master. I was disappointed to discover many years later that ORJ had joined Mary Whitehouse's Festival of Light, an organisation I considered misguided and at times preposterously narrow-minded. He later became its national director.

When I was in my early twenties, ORJ agreed to write a testimonial for me, to support my application for my first teaching post. He invited me to pick up the testimonial at his home in Ranmoor, one Sunday afternoon. He gave me tea and biscuits, and we had a hilarious hour, I telling stories about University life, about teaching practice, he about the school. He played a trick on me by writing a spoof reference and handing it to me, with an earnest, deadpan face, in a sealed envelope. As I stood to leave, he said: 'wouldn't you like to read what I've said? You might not like it.' I opened the envelope and fell about laughing at what he had written. This was the real ORJ. He gave me the real testimonial, we shook hands and said goodbye and farewell.

An account of my experience at the school would not be complete without a word about the man in charge of the operation, the headmaster, NL Clapton, 'Nat' to us. Nat arrived at the school the year before I did and, during all the seven years that I was there, he spoke to me only twice, once when he summoned me to his office, as I recounted previously, to fine me one shilling. The second time was in my upper sixth year, and the conversation went as follows:

'Foster?'

'Yes, sir.'

'I see you are intending to apply to St Cat's.'

'Yes, sir.'

'Well, if you must, but I wouldn't be too sanguine.'

He gave me no reasons, and I wondered what blood had to do with the matter but intuited that in this case sanguine meant optimistic. I looked it up in the OED. I was not wrong.

Nat, who appeared to have a permanent scowl, was a hefty man, slow-moving, sluggish almost, although still in his forties when I first set eyes on him. I read that he was a keen climber as a younger man. It was not evident. He often caught the same bus to school as I did, the number 8 circular bus. I used to look out for him at the bus stop outside his house in Nether Edge and, if he boarded the bus, I would lower my eyes to avoid his Medusan glower. One morning, I miscalculated and was forced to mumble 'morning, sir'. The response was the minimal raising of one eyebrow above the Billy Bunter spectacles and an almost imperceptible nod. To be fair to Clapton, his obituary speaks of him as a kind, hard-working, highly intelligent man, who hated standing on ceremony. I have no quibble with hard-working; it may well have been all work and no play that brought him to an early grave, at the age of 64, but I found no trace of kindness in the man. To me he was always remote, unapproachable and to be avoided at all costs.

I am conscious that I have not yet found a moment to speak about pals I made at the school. To be frank, I recall no firm friendships struck in my early years at the school. I think I considered that my handful of friends were at home in Heeley, and that King Edward's was just a passing phase in my existence, a place I went to in the daytime. I do remember spending a great deal of my free time in the second form with two serious boys, called Hawley and Turner. We were boys who took our own sandwiches to school and so ate lunch in the same classroom. Hawley and I played hundreds of games of chess, at any free moment of the day, with a scrap of paper, a pencil and a rubber. We sketched out a chessboard on a scrap of lined paper, pencilled in the symbols for the pieces, erasing them when we wanted to move them to another square. One day per week we went to lunchtime chess club. In the summer term, Hawley's pal, Turner, joined us, and our little triumvirate played cricket up against a wall in the school yard. Turner was a very unlikely-looking athlete, being round, pale and a little flabby, but he knew how to bowl leg-breaks and was developing a promising googly. He also owned the bat.

The third form was when I finally broke into the school football team, the Under 14s. I wore glasses and was not tall enough or powerful enough to be considered a centre forward, my position in the Lynwood House team. Josh White and Squirt Newsome were well established as inside right and right wing, which teachers seemed to consider my proper position. I did play quite a few matches that year, probably at Squirt's expense, and this meant I could be attached to the in-crowd of sporty boys, including Challenger, McAteer and Evison, who played a daily match on the slope leading down to the swimming pool. Or rather, they knew who I was. A tennis ball was all we were allowed, which demanded a special kind of skill unrelated to real football. To my mum's chagrin, it also led to a lot of scuffed shoes. It was in the Under 14s that my enduring, telepathic relationship with Bug Pike was first established. He was Hoddle to my Waddle, had a wand of a left foot, and floated long diagonal passes into my path for me to shoot the ball home. Off the pitch, we were not close, although coincidentally we did share digs at Uni. Until my A level years, I had no special friends, was part of no in-group, nor did I have enemies. I was neither sporty boy, nor swot, I got along with everyone, but if I had disappeared one day, I reckon no-one would have noticed, or minded much.

There were two recreational activities that took up inordinate amounts of my time during my first three years at the school. One was our form of shove-ha'penny, played on the wide window-sills of the first-floor corridor and an obsession with smaller boys. The two pennies represented opposing football teams, the ha'penny was the ball. We used a six-inch ruler to hit the penny onto the ha'penny and shoot through the goal at the end of the window-sill. It was highly regulated with strict rules of play, and was so absorbing that even I, a goody two shoes, was occasionally late for lessons. I confess that Bug Pike and I also whittled away a few evenings playing an expanded version of the game on Mrs Bissett's dining-table in our fresher year at Leeds.

The second game, played outside, against the end wall of the school building, had no name, but was a version of fives played with the feet and a tennis ball. The school had a fives court, a nod in the direction of Eton, Rugby and co, establishments which grammar schools often attempted to emulate, or simply imitate. The fives court, a sort of brick-built, open-air squash court, was practically never used, except for the annual school tournament, which I entered once, in the fifth form. I was eliminated in Round 1, emerging with a very bruised hand and resolving never to repeat the experience. The game closely resembled squash or pelota, but was played using the hand instead of a racket. Our nameless foot-ball game, against the school wall, was a sort of democratisation or dumbing down of fives. It was played in singles or doubles, contestants kicking the ball in turn, one-touch style, as it rebounded from the very long wall, until someone failed and lost the point. As several of these games were often played simultaneously and it was all taking place in the school yard, negotiating traffic and coping with unexpected deflections was a key skill. I loved it.

As we grow up, we begin to develop our own distinct identity. Birds of a feather do flock together, and I flocked together with Rad, Bro and Ogg – Roger Milner, Graham Brothers and Michael Ogglesby. Bro and Rad were in my English literature group, but my path never crossed Ogg's in the classroom at any stage of my school career, and I have no idea which subjects he was studying. He and I knew each other through being in Lynwood House, I suppose. If I were to categorise our little group, I would say we were slightly nonconformist, in other words we saw through some of the establishment cant without being overtly rebellious. Instinctively pragmatists, we swam along with the tide, making no waves. In 2021 terms, we were a small social bubble. Affable, unassuming and nonchalant were adjectives that might have been applied to us, but arrogant, ostentatious and 'cool' we were not. My three pals were all genuinely nice lads, and that's why I liked them. Bro was calm, unflurried, unhurried, competent, and a cross-country runner of some considerable ability. Ogg was more intense and a fine athlete, muscular, powerful. He engineered Lynwood's first ever victory in the house athletics competition, by persuading our competitors to practise on the close[46] for their event, and by employing a clever bunching strategy in the house cross-country race. He also, generously and regularly, lent me his Sexton Blake magazines, for which he was an enthusiastic advocate. I read them out of loyalty to Ogg, but secretly preferred John Steinbeck. Bro and Ogg were, each in his own way, self-contained, apparently in need of no-one's approval. Rad was easy-going, indolent, but smart. As well as English literature, he was studying economics and British Constitution, whilst continuing to wrestle with O level French, at which he had already had four or five fruitless stabs.

We acquired a certain amount of notoriety by setting up a harmless, lunchtime solo whist school, which was viewed with suspicion by certain teachers, as a sign of deep-seated moral turpitude. For us it was innocent, merely a pleasant and intelligent way of passing the long lunchtime break between lessons. News of our depravity eventually reached the ears of Senior Management, and the wily old bird SV 'Sammy' Carter, Second Master, whose sole function in the school was to lurk benevolently and whom I always found very affable, bearded me in the corridor, jovially, I thought: Was I one of the card crew? How much had I won today? I

---

[46] *Another nod in the direction of the public school ('There's a breathless hush in the close tonight', etc). The close was the large area of grass in front of the school.*

winked at him - outrageous of me, I know, but as I said, I quite liked him and felt he was on our side. Only about half a crown today, sir. Actually, no money ever changed hands, it was competitive, admittedly, but in a spirit of fun. Sammy said nothing, but the next day we heard on the grapevine that cards were forbidden.

We mooched around at lunchtime for a week or two, and then Rad had the brilliant idea of bringing in a set of dominoes. We took to spending the lunchtime break out of sight and mind in our form room on the first floor, Gerry's room, where we instituted a highly competitive fives and threes doubles tournament, playing every day until the end of the school year. I recorded the state of play daily at close of play, in the back of my French vocabulary book; the tournament winners were the first team to notch up a hundred victories. We completed several cycles of this absorbing ritual. We were disturbed only once, when a teacher, Bert Towers, opened the door, poked his head into the classroom and gasped in disgust, as though he had caught us *in flagrante delicto* in the throes of some lewd debauchery. His voice cracking with emotion, he spat at us 'you're incorrigible!'. Like you, we were mystified.

Another form in which our rebellious attitude revealed its ugly head was our custom of playing a word game in our 'free periods' in the library, which was reserved for private study only, but unsupervised. It was a simple game, but mildly entertaining and passed many a half-hour that could have been wasted preparing an essay or reading a dull book. To be fair to us, there was a lot of imaginative thinking and head-scratching involved. Each of us in turn said a letter of the alphabet. If you offered a letter that completed a word of four letters or longer, you were eliminated. If the previous player suggested a letter that you thought made it impossible to form a word, you challenged him. The decision was referred to the OED, our Bible. Arthur Dungworth, somewhat socially dysfunctional, in other words a pain in the neck, had shown an interest in our dominoes school, even as a spectator or a substitute player, but we had fobbed him off, and told him we considered him undesirable and unworthy of our company. He took to joining in our word game, a move which we countered by plotting together to spell abstruse or recondite words like yggdrasil, xoanon or zedoary, when Arthur was sitting in fourth position, and so would be eliminated immediately. Rad started the custom of treating Arthur as though he had some form of plague. He gave us all a leaf to keep with our bus pass. The idea was that whenever Arthur approached, we were to take out the leaf and hold it up in front of our faces, like garlic against a vampire, and say 'unclean! leaf! leaf!' Our persecution of Arthur was carried out in an apparently jocular manner, and he took it well enough, but although he was admittedly a pest at times, in all honesty it was unfair. Boys can be cruel.

I should confess one further peccadillo, a crime far more heinous than any in which we were rumbled. Sometimes, when we were free after break in the afternoon, Rad and I would sneak out of school to the snooker hall and play a couple of frames, which was all we could afford. We were indeed incorrigible, for I don't suppose either of us lost a moment's sleep lamenting our transgression.

This is a memoir, not an autobiography. Nevertheless, it is appropriate to say what became of my other three musketeers, in particular Rad. At the end of the upper sixth, Bro went off to university, I have no idea where. I never saw him again. Ogg's father, a disciplinarian, packed him off to join the South African police. I hope his immortal soul survived. The relationship between the three of us was based on solidarity and camaraderie, but was not sentimental, and we neither exchanged addresses nor attempted to keep in touch. In contrast, Rad and I were by now already close friends, and although we lived at opposite ends of the city, two bus routes apart, we spent a lot of our free time together, even to the extent of calling on each other impromptu. We had no phones. We formed a tightknit foursome with our two girlfriends, at weekends and in holidays. He and I went to the same university, although this was unplanned and by pure chance. He had finally nailed O level French and as a result had been offered a late place at Leeds, to study sociology and anthropology. In our last two terms, we finally shared a student house and then remained friends throughout our lives, at times drifting apart for a year or two, through geography or neglect, but always gravitating back to each other, often through our common soft spot for Sheffield Wednesday. Throughout the decades we often blundered into hilarious scrapes together. I was Stan to his Ollie, and appropriately our very last joint excursion, at his suggestion, was to the gloriously and hilariously dismal Laurel and Hardy Museum at Ulverston, Stan's birthplace. Rad died during the 2020 lockdown. His wife Pat invited me to his funeral in Darlington, as an honorary member of the family, and entrusted me with his eulogy. It was a hot day, and I drove to Darlington in shorts, pink shorts. I planned to change in the car park, into my navy linen jacket, pink shirt, red tie, and smart-casual trousers. On arrival, I discovered that I had left my trousers at home. There were no shops open and, in any case, there was no time for shopping. Another fine mess. I was mortified, but it turned out to be an entirely fitting finale to our special friendship. When Rad's daughter arrived, and I confessed that I had no trousers, she burst out laughing and said simply: 'Dad will love this!'

It had somehow always been assumed that I was one of the many who would sit the entrance exams at Oxford and Cambridge, in the autumn of 1957. It was decided that my destination was to read Modern Languages at Oxford, and the subliminal message was that go anywhere else was failure. We were each assigned to apply to a particular Oxford college, some boys to their father's old college, others to their teacher's colleges, where strings were to be discreetly pulled. The rest of us were randomly assigned to the remaining colleges. In the lucky dip I drew Pembroke, where I was sole occupier of palatial, if cold and draughty student quarters in the magnificent but intimidating Old Quad. The exams took place in a cavernous hall, containing hundreds of boys, all competing for scholarships and 'exhibitions' at Pembroke, Worcester and two other colleges. Between exams there was a short interview with a single, friendly academic, who posed bland questions like 'why are you applying to Pembroke?'. After the exams I was astonished to find that I was on the short list of eight boys listed for a second interview, at scary 30-minute intervals.

Imagine the scene. It is my first ever serious interview and I have no idea what to expect. I only know that it is important to present myself as interesting and rounded, special even, in order to single me out from the herd. I think I managed the last part at least. I found myself in a surreal circle of seven people, the other six all robed academics. When asked to speak about my extracurricular activities, I foolishly revealed my amateur dramatic performances in the church hall, hoping to project interesting and rounded. They asked me to specify which plays and which roles. They were probably expecting Shakespeare or, at a pinch, Sheridan, and I spotted some disconcerting eye-rolling when I confessed to the unsophisticated amdram kitsch served up by the Heeley St Peter's players. I felt I was one-nil down from the kick-off. We moved on to my German literature reading, which was extensive, and I should have been on firm ground. I had hoped to be asked about the *Sturm und Drang* lads - I loved their rebellious flavour and had written a couple of sound essays on them - but by now I was suffering from incipient brain-freeze, the conversation was out of control, and the scene had turned into a Kafkaesque nightmare. The rest is a blur, but I do remember that we ended on the *Gretchen am Spinnrade* episode in Goethe's *Faust,* which I loved because it contained Gretchen's broken-hearted lament and reminded me of so many love-songs and of emotions I could empathise with. It was real to me, and I should have said so. Unnerved by having already revealed my uncultured self with the amdram gaffe, I muttered instead that it was a bit like a traditional *Volkslied*, a comment I had read somewhere but only half understood, and the dons chatted for a while amongst themselves about the *Volkslied* genre, before releasing me back into the wild. Unsurprisingly, considering that I was outperformed at the interview by my new tie, I was offered no scholarship, no exhibition, no place, no crumb of comfort. Boys were not meant to cry in those days, and I didn't, but humiliation is an experience that eats into your soul and stays with you for good.

Shortly afterwards I fell victim to appendicitis, followed by one of those horrible infections you can pick up in hospital, where I was confined for three weeks. I missed the Cambridge entrance exams, which was probably a blessing in disguise, and accepted the first university place I was offered.

In writing this memoir, I may well have given an overall negative impression of my time at KES, and indeed it could have been so much better. The school may well have prided itself on its liberal education, its intention to produce well-rounded young men, *mens sana in corpore sano*, but it was essentially an intellectual sausage factory for producing academics capable of passing public examinations, with the ultimate goal of sending as many boys as possible to Oxbridge, and preferably Oxford. In hindsight, crashing through the O level curriculum in four years, including highly inadequate science provision and negligible concession to creative areas, falls far short of a rounded education. Broad, creative and liberal education was sacrificed to early specialisation. Already in the second form I was learning three foreign languages and no longer had lessons in religious education, music, or art; geography and woodwork were the next to go at the end of that year. This is not to deny that there were outstanding opportunities to participate in public performances of music and drama, to play in school sports teams or participate in extracurricular societies like chess or debating. The school accepted only very able boys and was interested only in excellence; there was little room in its heart for mediocrity. [47]

The picture was by no means entirely negative. There were indeed attempts to broaden our horizons, whilst keeping us busy. I have already mentioned the additional provision for us young A level students in the fifth form, the European history with Daddy Collins and the general classical literature with Marcus. In addition, we studied for a further O level qualification in Scripture, provided by the excellent RA Summers, who was meticulously well prepared, professional and inspirational, and most notably made no attempt to impress upon us the merits of Christianity. I had no idea that studying the Acts of the Apostles and the gospel of St Luke could be so fascinating. He treated us as adults, as serious theology students, and we responded accordingly.

---

[47] *My one and only appearance in the school play was as a Roman soldier, in Shaw's Caesar and Cleopatra. I had one line, and I spoke it beautifully, in a Cockney accent, which I was quite proud of: 'Do not tantalise a poor man'. The audience tittered pleasingly. I came off stage, relieved at having carried out my nerve-racking role, only to be upbraided for forgetting to remove my spectacles. I was mocked for months afterwards, by both boys and masters, as the bespectacled Roman soldier.*

I must forgive King Edward's its faults; it was a creation of its time, and after all I was proud enough to say that it was my school. Our education was far from perfect, and there were many boys whom it served badly and whose potential it fell far short of fulfilling, but at least it opened doors for boys like me who survived it, doors into an academic world that I would have found beyond my reach, and to a job that I loved.

IX Teenage years: St Valentine and St Silas

Meanwhile, off-campus, real life was happening, right here in Heeley, mostly in Heeley St Peter's Mission Church hall. I'm not sure when teenage life proper actually began, but it was probably when I was about fourteen.

In the yard behind the lamppost on the lane there were two houses. In the left-hand one lived Eunice Morley, who was a schoolmate of our June. Unlike June, Eunice had not gone to college, but instead had an office job and went to work dressed very smartly. The reason I mention Eunice is that I saw her walking up the lane one day with a girl whose name I knew to be Muriel, but about whom I knew nothing more except that she was the same age as I and lived in the same yard as Eunice. I thought what a fine pair they looked, Eunice and Muriel, chatting happily together. What I actually was thinking was that I liked the cut of Muriel's jib.

'Hello, Eunice,' I said. Eunice smiled back at me and said hello, but Muriel blanked me.

That night in bed I hatched a cunning plan to inveigle myself into Muriel's good books. Before I go into detail, I would advise any young man who is interested in learning how to ensnare a member of the opposite sex to pay very close attention to what I'm about to say. Using my infallible techniques, with minor adjustments here and there, success will be guaranteed. To continue, the next time our paths crossed on the lane, Muriel and mine, I planned to say 'Hello, Muriel, which school do you go to?' The second time, I would advance with a more adventurous salvo: 'I went to the pictures last night. Doris Day.' And if she looked at all interested, I would ask if she liked Doris Day. That would probably be enough for our second conversation. Softly, softly, catchee monkey. The third time, I would be much bolder and tell her that I was going to the pictures again tonight and then mention the star of the picture, which I would have researched. After that, I presumed that we would fall into an easy conversation and become pals. Then the sky would be the limit.

I had learnt from Hollywood pictures, at least from the love-story kind, that it was the modest, self-effacing fellow, who was kind to animals and old ladies, who got the girl in the end, not the obviously handsome type who swept women off their feet with his Errol Flynn ways. At least, that was the case with the Doris Day type of girl, and I was not very interested in the Marilyn Monroes, as they were a bit scary. It was Doris Day for me, every time.

In the event, my path crossed Muriel's very rarely, even though she did live just across the lane, and when I did bump into her on rare occasions, she ignored me and walked straight past me, looking down at her feet. Perhaps she was shy too. Or perhaps she thought I was a specky-four-eyes twerp. The closest we came to communication of any kind was when we saw each other face-to-face from our respective bedroom windows one school morning. Muriel snatched her curtains and drew them to, quicker than I could say Jack Robinson. It was like the Lady of Shallot. I wondered if her mirror crack'd from side to side.

By now I had lost interest in Muriel anyway. I had given my heart to another, at the youth club in the church hall, although I was still using the same infallible keep-my-distance technique to ensnare the object of my desire.

Her name was Sylvia. She was a few months older than I and therefore already fifteen. She was pretty, had blonde, short hair, probably dyed, lived on the next street to me, and went to Rowlinson School, like Miffer (who we now called Ray), Tommy Broomhead and one or two others. I had first noticed her running around the church hall on a youth club evening, chased by two boys. Youth club was on Wednesdays and was nothing more than a venue for teenagers to hang out and chill, although none of us knew the expressions 'hang out' and 'chill' at the time, and so I presume we didn't really know what we were doing. I certainly did not. Sylvia appeared to have 'personality', a quality much admired by boys, and so she was much sought after by my peers. She had a boyfriend called Dave, also at Rowlinson School. Dave did not come to the youth club, as he lived at Gleadless Town End, some distance away. I had seen Dave once. He bore a close resemblance to Dean Martin, which was a bit of a snag, as I did not look like any film star that I knew.

I had never spoken to Sylvia, nor she to me, but she did once smile at me, which was encouraging at least. The situation continued for some weeks, past my fifteenth birthday, which I felt put me in a better position to be a candidate for her affections, although I did not hold out much hope of pressing my suit. One morning, I was a little late leaving for school, and whom should I see hurrying past the end of Carrfield Lane? You have guessed. It was Sylvia, in her school uniform, which looked a little tatty, and white ankle socks. Nevertheless, this did not detract too much from her feminine charms and actually made her seem more attainable. I hurried to catch up with her, accidentally of course, but she was a fast walker and seemed to be in a rush. By the time I had almost caught up with her, I was out of breath and decided to abandon our accidental meeting after all and stay at a safe distance behind, observing how beautifully she skipped along and how attractively her satchel swung from her shoulder. As we reached the bottom of Gleadless Road, she turned her head and saw me: 'Oh, hello!' she said. I am fairly certain that I blushed: 'Catch my bus here', I explained, pointing towards my bus stop.

That was our first conversation, but it was a point of entry, a foot in the door, Pyramus and Thisbe's crack in the wall. At the next youth club, she said hello to me again, and I had a subject for a conversation. It turned out that she had been on her way down Gleadless Road to catch her school bus at Heeley Bottom, which she did every day, and which was where I caught the circular bus to King Ted's. A connection!

From then on, I would lurk every morning in the bay window and watch out for her to hurry past the end of Northcote Road. She was very often late, and then I would have to race off at lightning speed to arrive hot and sweaty in time for the half past eight bus, which got me to school with seconds to spare before Sammy locked the school doors and began to funnel the latecomers up the grand main stone staircase to sign the late book. These few seconds were crucial, as I had a proud record of never being late and did not want to besmirch it. My normal practice was to catch the ten past eight, to arrive comfortably with plenty of time to spare before registration, but Sylvia had turned me into one of Sammy's 'last minute crew' who flirted daily with the late book.

This, my fourth year at grammar school and my O level year, was also the year of the 15th birthday parties. There was a group of us always invited to each other's party, which followed a fixed pattern: orange squash, lemonade, ham and tongue sandwiches, trifle, birthday cake with candles, followed by Postman's Knock. For those readers who are unfamiliar with the concept of Postman's Knock, I shall explain. One boy or girl, beginning for example with the birthday girl, was sent to sit on the stairs. We boys were allocated a number, randomly. A bossy person, usually a flirty girl, then shouted three questions through the door to the birthday girl: 'What number? How many letters? How many stamps?' The number indicated the lucky boy, the letters the number of kisses she would give, the stamps the number of times that she could stamp on his foot. Each answer was given by the required number of knocks on the door, three knocks meaning Number 3 boy, and so on. Most stamps on the foot were delivered gently, unless the girl was in a bad mood or disliked the lad. The kisses varied in quality and duration, depending on a variety of factors.

The process then continued, in the form of a continuous chain, the boy remaining on the stairs, new numbers allocated, and so on, until we got bored. If it sounds like Sodom and Gomorrah, then I assure you it was not, at least not in my experience. I can't say that I enjoyed it very much, as not only did I find the whole business embarrassing, but any kisses I received tended to be either peremptory pecks on the cheek, or, if they were on the mouth, tended to be wet and unpleasant, what my mum called 'sloppy kisses'. No tongues were ever involved, thank goodness. When I was lucky enough to be chosen by a girl I quite 'liked', I was far too self-conscious to profit from the opportunity. What I really wanted was for my turn to coincide with Sylvia, but she was not always invited to these parties, and when she was, it just didn't happen.

Sylvia's morning timekeeping was erratic, and despite my daily bay window vigil, my success rate in 'bumping into' her on the way to school was no better than one in five. However, I was a persistent suitor. At a discreet distance. Eventually, my policy paid off, much to my astonishment.

One Sunday in June, the Sunday School held its annual summer party in Meersbrook Park, and we youth club lot were invited to join with the little kids, for a picnic. It was here that Miffer took me aside confidentially and told me that Sylvia had told Pam to tell Val to tell Ray, who was Val's boyfriend, that she would like to 'go out' with me, which meant be my girlfriend. I saw her waiting under a tree, looking towards me. I told Miffer to tell Val to tell Pam to tell Sylvia 'yes'. I did not add that Barkiss was willing, although I thought it.

Our first evening of 'going out' together was deliciously uncomfortable, as I remember it. We asked each other questions, she told me that she would have to go to Dave's and tell him she was going to chuck him, and it would not be easy. I asked her why some boys shouted 'Flat-Patch' after her sometimes, and she blushed and explained that the nickname was from before she had a bosom. I exhibited a correct amount of shock, I think, and reassured her that her bosom was now perfectly adequate. I did not ask her why she preferred me to Dave, but I did wonder. There were several kisses, superior in quality to the Postman's Knock variety. Sylvia was a very good kisser, as I knew she would be, and I turned out to have hidden talent too.

The next day, Ray Smith was a bit off-hand with me, because Dave was one of his pals at school. The course of true love never did run smooth.

Sylvia and I swore undying love and eternal fidelity, agreed we would marry and have a family together, and for several years we were an item, until she broke my heart ruthlessly, then took me back, and then broke it again. Something I thought would last forever had been snuffed out like a candle, squashed like a fly on a window-pane, thrown away like a used bus ticket.

Centre of picture, Sylvia, 1957

Miffer and I, acting daft, 1956

If I now seem to reflect at all flippantly on these teenage amours and these broken hearts, then I may have given the reader a false impression of the pain involved. I should add therefore that I have also had a broken arm, which was far quicker to heal and gave me only two sleepless nights.

And yes, she did dye her hair.

†

And now I come to a second teenage romance, one which abides until today, my love affair with the archetypal English game, cricket.

When we are little boys we do crazy things, have crazy obsessions. Among mine were BRS spotting, Subbuteo (more of that later), collecting colourful cigarette packets, and tiddlywinks football. I have already told how BRS spotting took me on a train journey far more exciting than any embarked on by Michael Portillo and his Baedeker, to the far-flung fields of Doncaster and the A1. The cigarette packet collecting was perhaps stranger still. I would search the gutters and pavements of Heeley, Meersbrook and Woodseats for rare and beautiful examples like *Churchman No 1, Churchman No 2, State Express 555, Passing Clouds* (my all-time favourite), De Reske (the 'Aristocrat of Cigarettes'), and my prime exhibit, the gorgeously exotic Egyptian brand, *Simon Arzt*, which promised faraway places and mystery. I gathered an extensive collection, the more beautiful and pristine the better. Once I even took the bus to Fulwood, which I knew to be a posher district and therefore likely to have more upmarket discarded packets on its prosperous pavements, but I was to be disappointed, and my day out was in vain. There was lamentably far less litter, and pickings were thin. What happened to my world-beating collection I shall never know. Perhaps my mum threw it out, absent-mindedly, with the back copies of the *Star*, not realising that it would probably be worth millions by now, like my priceless stamp collection, borrowed by the faithless Sylvia and never returned. I am not bitter.

The tiddlywinks football was a game that I invented and played alone while Mum and Dad were out ballroom dancing with Connie and Arnold Wilde on Thursday evenings at the Manor Social Club. My field of play was the kitchen table, covered in the plush table-cloth which was normally reserved for company, but provided a perfect replica of the famous Wembley greensward. My goals were two Bakelite egg cups lying on their side, their goalkeepers large marbles, shiny globbies. The ball was a small tiddlywink and the players were represented by a large tiddlywink[48]. From there on, the rules of the game become somewhat arcane, and so I shall spare the general reader the details, but it always began with the draw for the third round of the FA Cup, using 64 slips of paper and Dad's cap. Surprisingly, although I always played out each of the 63 ties with scrupulous impartiality, Sheffield Wednesday triumphed quite often in the Final.

Some obsessions, as I have already confessed in the first half of this chapter, become affairs of the heart, and so it was with my fascination for cricket. From a very young age my summers were filled with cricket, watching my dad's team every Saturday and often in midweek, following the fortunes of Yorkshire and spending a day at Bramall Lane watching my heroes, whenever I could.

And so, unsurprisingly, another solitary pursuit of mine was the cricket game, *OWZAT*, which I played using a hexagonal pencil, with numbers and words scratched on, in place of the official chunky hexagonal long dice. At first, I would fabricate a scorecard out of a scrap of paper or cardboard, but then Mum bought me a proper scorebook for my birthday, from Jack Archer's on Bramall Lane, and I used that, marking down every single ball bowled, every roll of the dice. I played county matches, Test matches, matches between my dad's team and England, and later, as a sophisticated Leeds University freshman, I invented whimsical contests between philosophers and dictators, symphonists and novelists, or Old Testament against eleven disciples (with Judas as 12th man). Eventually, I acquired an authentic *OWZAT* set, second-hand, but by then my enthusiasm for the game had faded a little.

---

[48] *I am not a connoisseur of tiddlywinks, but I do understand that they are officially called 'winks' and 'squidgers'.*

Little Cricket was possibly my own invention, although admittedly there is nothing new under the sun. I thought what a good idea it would be to fashion a small wooden cricket bat and to play a miniature game of cricket, using a marble as the ball and a Swan Vesta's matchbox as the wickets. I spent hours playing this game on my own, my left hand bowling to my right hand and vice versa. Eventually I persuaded other lads to play with me and I spent many an afternoon playing with cousins Robert and Jimmy. In our game, there was no LBW, as this was impossible to judge, and so Jimmy cheated outrageously, blocking every difficult delivery with the back of his hand. Consequently, we could never get him out, much to Robert's frustration. The sibling rivalry between the two was intense, as was the competitive instinct of the pair of them. Our games finally had to stop when Jimmy fired the marble across their front room and smashed the glass in his mum's china cabinet. Six and out.

Saturday, June 5, 1954 was my cricket red letter day. That afternoon I had been playing cricket in Graves Park for two or three hours with my two pals, Ray Smith and Albert Wood. Teatime was calling, and our game was drawing to an end. Marching towards us from the direction of the pitch where Dad's team used to play came a small man in cricket flannels, with wispy, sandy hair: 'Would any of you chaps like a game, we're one short.'

Although I was a mad keen cricketer, I had never played in a proper game of cricket. I was intimidated by the school team set-up, which I thought was reserved for posh lads with their own kit, flannels, pads and bats. But this seemed like a nice man, I was excited and agreed to play. Miffer said he would tell my mum I would be late home. My team's innings was coming to an end, and I was sent into bat at number 10 in my shorts and plimsolls, an outrageously large pair of pads and flimsy batting gloves with rubber spikes on the back, but at least I had my own bat, even if it was a bit small for me now. I did not score any runs, but I did manage to make contact with the ball several times. I think the bowlers were very kind to me, as was the wicketkeeper who warned me that I kept on standing outside my ground and that some other teams would have run me out. When my batting partner was caught out, the nice man with the wispy, sandy hair came in to bat at number 11, and we made a few more runs before I was bowled out.

The next match was on the following Monday afternoon, Whit Monday, at 3 o'clock against Hooton Roberts. Was I available? Was I available! I was available all right! Even though I had been looking forward to going to Doncaster Races with Mum and Dad, I agreed to play without giving it a second thought. But did I have flannels and boots – and white socks? asked the skipper. I said I could borrow Dad's. I was to meet the team in the queue for the Doncaster bus in Pond Street, coincidentally the same queue Mum and Dad would be in. My new skipper introduced himself to Mum and Dad and shook Dad's hand firmly. "Don't worry, Mr and Mrs Foster, we'll look after young John here, he's a promising lad'. I soon found out that everybody was a promising lad to the skipper.

The nice man with the wispy, sandy hair was Willis B Seton, who liked to be called Bill, and the team St Silas Imps CC, my own team from that day onwards, for the next two decades. Throughout my teens, my student years in Leeds, my years in Ashby de la Zouch; wherever I was, I came back to Sheffield to play for the Imps on a Saturday afternoon.

That afternoon at Hooton Roberts, I was fielding at midwicket, and the ball was hit hard towards me. I dived forward at full length and caught it. The outfield at Hooton Roberts was a farmer's field, complete with cowpats, and the grass long and lush. I stood up with the ball in both hands, along with quite a few blades of grass. The batsman walked off, I was congratulated by my team-mates and felt very proud, as well as surprised at my own catching skill. The skipper interrogated me. Had I caught it cleanly? Yes, I thought so, but it had all happened in a flash. 'Young John here's not sure', called Bill to the umpire and then ran to the pavilion to fetch the batsman back in. Young John here felt a little bit cheated, but this small scene was a microcosm of the great sporting gentleman that was Bill Seton. He was the most scrupulous man I ever came across, and as I believe has often been said of far lesser men, when God made Bill Seton, He broke the mould. As my teammate and dentist, David Ibrahim, once commented to me: 'It embarrasses Bill when we win, his favourite result is when we only just lose.' There was more than a grain of truth in David's cynicism. Bill loved a close sporting contest and was always very keen to 'give them (our opponents) a good game'. Once when we skittled a team out for 30-odd, he reversed our batting order to give the opponents a chance (apart from himself, who remained at No 11, of course). The match ended before tea, at about half past four, with Bill and me footling around for ten runs to scrape home. But my, oh my, was he pleased that day!

We played our home games at the far side of Concord Park, where our wicket, although beautifully prepared like all parks pitches in Sheffield, was at the top of a steep slope, and so woe betide the boundary fielder on the low side who missed the ball and faced the long trek to fetch it back.

A more motley crew than the St Silas Imps team you could not imagine. The two Bills, Seton and Bradshaw, were the organisers and motors of the club. Bill Seton was the admin man who arranged all fixtures, sent every player a weekly postcard with directions for the next fixture, and also captained the team. Billy Bradshaw, of a similar vintage, looked after the kit, such as it was; he kept it in his shed and brought it to the matches on his motorbike and sidecar. Billy had a leather helmet and gauntlets which made him look like a driver from Wacky Races. He was also very short and extremely bowlegged, often a handicap for a wicket-keeper, which he was. Another handicap for Billy was his equipment. He had to wear a strange contraption, fastened by straps around his waist and between his buttocks, which looked like an exhibit from a mediaeval chastity belt museum. This 'keeper's box', as it was known, was a most uncomfortable and unyielding piece of underwear. I can attest to its discomfort from my experience of substituting for Billy when he was indisposed. His wicket-keeping gloves also were museum pieces and had become stiffer, harder, and thinner over the years, so that they were now no longer suitable for either catching the ball or for protecting the hands. Roger Milner and I took to calling them the dustbin lids. It was a minor miracle when Billy caught the ball cleanly, and fielding at first slip I lost count of the number of times I took a catch deflected from Billy's dustbin lids.

Despite these handicaps, Billy was a very competent wicket-keeper, and his unprepossessing appearance disguised a sharp wit and a wry sense of humour. I liked him very much. He was also a stolid and stubborn opening batsman, whose speciality was to bore the opposition into a stupor. He was the polar opposite of Freddie Marshall, our star batsman. Freddie was a brilliant cricketer, a batsman of very high quality who could have played for Yorkshire had he put his mind to it, and an even better fielder, with a throw like a tracer bullet, Australian style, whizzed in waist high. We were blessed that Freddie stayed and played with us, the Rag, Tag and Bobtail of cricket. One day in High Hazels Park, Freddie and Billy opened the innings. After two hours, we were 130 without loss, with Freddie on 110 and Billy on 7. We were beginning to jeer Billy affectionately by now, and I was sweaty-legged in my pads waiting to go in next. Billy took the hint, had a swing and was out. I went in, was out first ball, quickly followed by the rest of the team. We were all out for 150, and we lost.

Bill Seton was to me already an old man when I started to play for the Imps at 14 years old. I would guess he was in his late forties when I first met him. He had already been running the club for twenty years and was to carry on for another twenty. He was an excellent captain who exuded energy and professionalism and made us all feel as though we were proper cricketers. He encouraged us, kept us on our toes, retained the same dignity in victory and defeat, and was the only man I have known who truly regarded Triumph and Disaster as impostors. Whenever I was going out to bat and we were in a dire situation, Bill would murmur in my ear 'Cometh the hour, cometh the man, John', I would suddenly feel like Len Hutton and always raised my game. You see, he was not parodying himself, he was serious, and when this unimpressive-looking little man spoke, I learned to listen.

As a cricketer, he left a lot to be desired. Placing himself last in the batting order was not only typically unselfish, but entirely justified by his batting average. He never bowled. His fielding was hampered by having the top knuckle of one finger on each hand missing owing to accidents at work. He also could see very little from one eye. Nevertheless, his catching was sound. He was determined never to drop a catch, to the extent that he would lean back and allow the ball to first thud painfully into his chest before he snatched it with his hands. On one occasion Bill found himself under one of those steepling hits that take forever to plummet down out of the sun. The impact of the ball crashing into his breast bone knocked him flat on his back, but he made the catch.

Our kit was unmitigatedly and laughably lousy. It consisted of a bulky, dusty leather portmanteau containing three pairs of ancient, thin and floppy pads, which Billy Bradshaw whitened every close season whether they needed it or not, each with at least one buckle missing, a couple of old balls that Bill Seton had begged from somewhere (I do not remember us ever having a new ball), three pairs of ancient batting gloves, which you had to wind around your wrist a couple of times before attaching a sausage-shaped thumb piece, two much-repaired and taped-up bats, a set of stumps and bails, and last but not least Billy's chastity belt and dustbin lids. The club had no money, its players were all hard up, except perhaps David the dentist, and so we could never afford new kit. Our matchday subs of two shillings went towards paying for the hire of the pitch. After I had broken two fingers, I bought my own batting gloves, from Jack Archer's, of course.

Our opponents varied as much in quality as our own playing personnel. We never joined a league, and all our fixtures were friendly matches, against church teams, village teams, and league teams with a blank day, as well as high-quality opposition like Yorkshire Council teams. We played on parks pitches with wooden huts for changing rooms, on farmers' fields, on picturesque village greens and on classy grounds like Thoresby Hall and Rotherham Phoenix, with its grand pavilion and social club. And even showers.

Our team was a mixture of good cricketers, who could have played at a far higher level but who turned out for the Imps because Bill asked them to, and lads who just loved to play sport. There was the silent Roy Bland, who bowled off breaks and seemed to be rated highly by Bill, although many opposition batsmen had a different view. There was Tommy Littlewood, who sent down accurate, medium-paced seamers on a length and batted at number 10, sometimes right-handed, sometimes left-handed. I thought at first that this was just a whim or an excuse for getting out for a duck, but Tommy seemed genuinely unsure which was his stronger side and, in any case, proved to be equally useless with either hand. Walt Marshall, Freddie's brother, was in personality and ability completely different from the laconically droll Fred. He was the essence of ordinariness and bowled slow medium trundlers which kept the scoreboard moving along nicely, without ever threatening to take a wicket. Quite a few of my friends became regulars, notably David, my dentist friend, and Roger Milner, my friend from school. We were one or two short every week without fail, and I became Bill's agent in recruiting new young lads. Another of Bill's agents was Charlie Bird, a dopey fellow, who was such a bad cricketer that we were a better team if he forgot to come. Charlie ran a youth club and often turned up with a couple of waifs and strays who didn't know one end of the bat from the other. One regular member of Charlie's entourage was a lad who was always and only referred to as Young David. To my knowledge, Young David never spoke, except to his girlfriend, who came along as support. Nor did Young David ever score a run. This may all sound like coarse cricket to you the reader, but we took it all very, very seriously, and when we were finally old enough, we discussed it all long and hard in the pub afterwards.

As postscript to this teenage love affair, I should like to add that, as well as recruiting many pals and cousins over the years, as Bill's player agent, I also eventually recruited Mum and Dad. When I was 20 and Dad was 54, he came out of a long sporting retirement to help us out and played the second half of the season with the Imps, with some distinction, taking quite a number of wickets. Mum, who had been scorer for Dad's team, took over scorer duties. Dad and I batted together several times, and he usually did his best to run me out with his quick singles and risky twos. I am grateful for those moments. It was his last summer.

X Feast days and fun days

Then, as now, the major festival of the calendar year was Christmas. It was less of a commercialised festival in my childhood, and still retained a strong religious element. We knew the story of the angel Gabriel's visit, Mary, Joseph, the donkey, the long journey back to Bethlehem, the innkeeper, the stable, the manger, the animals, the wise men, and the shepherds, all in minute detail, and could sing off by heart a dozen or more carols. Nevertheless, it was, then as now, the time of year that we children looked forward to most of all, because there was the promised visit of Father Christmas and his eight reindeer – as far as I recall, Rudolph had not yet been recruited.

We children, however, had already realised the commercial possibilities of Christmas, long before Amazon.co.uk or John Lewis. On Christmas Eve, we went out, hatted, scarved and gloved, alone, in pairs or in small groups, to sing a couple of verses of a carol outside people's back door, wish them a Merry Christmas, knock on their door and demand money. The adults seemed to love it, clamoured for it even, often asked us inside to eat mince pies and sing more, usually with an even more generous gratuity. Cousin Geoff and I could trouser more in one evening than a whole year's pocket money.

One small snag, after the early boom years of carolling, was that we were obliged to take cousin Peter along with us. Whilst we loved him dearly, this did introduce a little grit into the well-oiled cogs of our operation. Peter had been damaged at birth and was severely mentally handicapped.

He was five years older than I and already had a surprisingly deep baritone voice. It was a miracle that Peter had learned any carol at all, but he *had* learned one verse of Good King Wenceslas. The result was that we had to sing the same song at every door. As Peter knew only one verse, he would repeat it while we were trying to sing verse 2. The effect was already peculiar, notwithstanding the conflicting lyrics, with its blend of Geoff's fledgling tweeting, my noble, melodic treble and a descant of Peter's tuneless, grunting baritone. Visually too, we were a motley trio. Geoff was tiny and Peter was very tall for his age. My feeling was that the quality of our Christmas offering suffered a good deal, not to mention its diminished commercial appeal. Our speed of movement between clients was also affected, and our coverage of the district was consequently less comprehensive. Not only were takings well down, but we now had to split them three ways. Nevertheless, I was very fond of Peter's dad, my Uncle Harry, and it was worth every penny of the lost revenue to make him happy by taking Peter along with us. Geoff also liked having Peter in the team and, in any case, he had not yet learned the value of money. He had twice already swallowed a threepenny bit – the chunky, twelve-sided sort – and had had to be hospitalised once, until it came out the other end.

Peter

I need not elaborate on the excitement of Christmas morning and waking to a stocking (later a pillow-case) bulging with presents from Mum and Dad, uncles and aunts. These Christmas delights are universal and timeless. In my stocking there were always an orange and some nuts, which I at once cast ungratefully and venally aside, not having as yet a fully developed sense of the importance of tradition. There were always boys' 'annuals' and football and cricket books from aunts and uncles, and the brilliant Rupert annuals that you could read twice, once through the picture-stories, once through the rhyming text. I loved them all and consumed the lot well before the end of January, most of them twice over. One year, when I was eight or nine, I had come across a story where a girl went into a little shop and longed for the books that she saw on the shelves but could only ever dream of reading, as her mother was a poor widow. By some miracle, I forget how, the books arrived in her stocking at Christmas. I made a note of the six books concerned and presented the list to Mum, requesting one of them for Christmas. The following Christmas morning they were *all* there, every single one, individually wrapped. How often life mimics art, I mused. It took a while to repress my feelings of guilt at being such a greedy and demanding son.[49]

One or two of the presents I opened on those Christmas mornings stand out as memorable. There was of course the famous 'casey' mentioned in a previous chapter, but the present that gave me most pleasure was a game I had seen advertised over and over in my weekly magazines, from about 1949 onwards. Every week I would seek out the advert, re-read the details and dream of possessing this wonderful table football game, with real players and goals and finger-tip control, which was publicised modestly in small print by a certain P.J. Adolph.

Now, I had more than once discovered that things advertised were often not what they were cracked up to be, and

---

[49] *The books were* Swiss Family Robinson, Masterman Ready, Treasure Island, Black Beauty, Robinson Crusoe, *and a sixth that I can't for the life of me recall.*

so, dreading disappointment and disillusion, but unable to contain my ardour a moment longer, I requested it for Christmas. Mum and Dad were sceptical, and I feared the worst, but on Christmas morning there it was, in a cubic box about 10 inches tall. Inside was a treasure trove of tiny cardboard players, one team in red, the other in blue. There were tiny goals and a plastic ball, which was ludicrously large in comparison, but what the heck! I spent half the morning fitting the players meticulously into the slots in their plastic bases. I was in heaven! Later on, I squandered my spending money on accessories like tiny shirt numbers to gum onto the players' backs, a luxury green baize pitch, and unbreakable plastic players in the colours of the Sheffield clubs. I even bought the cricket version of the game. I frivolled away myriad hours of the rest of my childhood and the majority of my teenage years on this tomfoolery. When I became a man, I put away childish things, but Subbuteo still lurks in the depths of my games-chest, and from time to time I still must strain to resist its siren song.

My most surprising Christmas present arrived on the Christmas before my 14th birthday. I woke to find a huge cardboard box, which I unpacked slowly and carefully. The box was very heavy, and unsurprisingly so, as it contained a 'cinematograph'. Previously, my parents had watched me admiring the 'magic lantern' at my Auntie Louie's house. Louie, or Louisa, was dad's younger sister, who lived in a new 'prefab' with all mod cons in East Bank Road. The magic lantern was a device which projected still images onto the wall of the living room. I had been fascinated by this brilliant new machine and had watched open-mouthed as a panoply of pictures appeared as if out of nowhere.

The cinematograph was a horse of a different colour; it projected *moving* pictures, just like at the Heeley Green! I was thrilled, and there were no words to describe my delight and pride of possession. The Fosters immediately became the envy of family and friends. We were the only known family to have such an extravagantly modern apparatus. People flocked to 16 Northcote Road to see the sensational device in action, to gasp in delight at the moving pictures projected onto a sheet suspended from the ceiling. There was no sound, if you don't count the whirring and clicking made by the machine. My new cinematograph was second-hand, of course, and with it came three cans of 16mm film: a silent Charlie Chaplin movie, with Chaplin in the role of a mean-spirited tramp, a Mickey Mouse cartoon involving mean-spirited hornets, and a military documentary entitled 'From El Alamein to Tunis'. This last film was, on first viewing, interesting for its historical content, but was in black and white, or sometimes sepia, very boring and showed little or no military action. It had a sporadically subtitled narrative. It was also very long, lasting about an hour and a half.

A certain level of skill, let us call it a knack, was required to operate the cinematograph, and I had acquired this knack through my experience of the tricky installation process involved in spooling *From El Alamein to Tunis*, Charlie and Micky around the complex pathway from reel to 'gate' to empty reel. The gate was the finicky part of the procedure and often gave trouble during the showing of a film, too often resulting in the film coming off track and piling up on the kitchen floor. Occasionally the film would jam and begin to melt and then break in the heat of the projector lamp, so that the molten celluloid needed to be cut out and the two ends joined. I had become the family expert in controlling the gate and its eccentricities.

Regrettably, after many sessions of watching the same films over and over, the cinematograph experience became tedious, our audiences dwindled, and we too lost interest in our technological miracle. It lay in its cardboard box, neglected, in a corner of my bedroom. Nevertheless, the cinematograph was eventually to find a new public and a second lease of life.

Fast forward two years to 1956. If you have been paying attention, you will remember that I am now paired up with the fair Sylvia. I have wasted no time in showing off my prize possession and my impressive spooling skills and gate control to my girlfriend. This has awoken a degree of interest among our circle of friends, in particular from Derek, the recently acquired boyfriend of our friend Pam. He is a couple of years older than us and a motor mechanic. I agree to put on a showing of the full range of my film library for his and Pam's delectation, on the night when Mum and Dad go dancing and the house will be free for teenage use. I should say at this point that these showings required complete disruption of the kitchen, the moving of furniture, the installation of easy chairs for my guests' comfort, the suspending of the sheet from the ceiling, but Derek is more than willing to help with these preparations, is delighted with the evening's entertainment and insists we repeat it asap. These cinematographic performances become a regular feature in our four lives. I wonder why Derek is so enthusiastic about the cinematograph and, it seems, especially for *From El Alamein to Tunis*. Perhaps he is an enthusiast for military documentaries or just for new technology in general. At any rate I am pleased to be popular.

In the end, the penny drops. Derek and Pam are not film buffs, nor is Derek particularly interested in military history. I have been far too occupied in gate control and general supervision of projection matters, and the whole operation is of course conducted in darkness. Sylvia remarks that our guests have not exactly been giving full attention to the screen. Their regular visits to my showings have been in the interests of smooching rather than cinematography. This becomes more evident when Derek acquires his own car and the film session requests come to an abrupt end.

A few years later, Pam and Derek married, and for all I know are happily married still. They did not invite me to their wedding, despite my having provided perfect conditions for their budding romance to flower by facilitating unlimited weekly canoodling opportunities, in the dark. On reflection, I feel I was used.

Christmas Day and Christmas dinner were always a family affair, a feast prepared by my mum and her sisters, Annie and Lily. Often, we would be joined by Auntie Eva and Uncle Tom, mum's brother, and occasionally another brother, Uncle Harry, with Auntie Winnie and Peter. You could always count on between 12 and 16 for Christmas dinner. To seat the multitude, we borrowed a trestle table and extra chairs from the church hall. It was a masterly feat of logistics by the women of the family to produce such a banquet in such cramped and spartan conditions. On one occasion only, the men donned aprons, cleared the table, and washed and dried the dishes. There was general chaos and hilarity, sexist humour being no doubt the theme. They were forbidden from repeating this service in the future.

Christmas Day evening was celebrated by party games, which I loved and looked forward to for weeks beforehand.

These games were only played at Christmas and did not vary from year to year, but were all the better for that. One game involved taking turns to toss a ping-pong ball into a chamber pot. If you could make it stay in – more difficult than you imagine - you scored a point. We knew how to have fun! There was always a break between games at some point in the evening, for a buffet featuring cold meats, pork pie, pickled onions and red cabbage, and of course Christmas cake and mince pies. The whole process was repeated at another sister's house on Boxing Day evening. New Year's Eve was similar, but with a later finish, marked by *Auld Lang Syne* and emotional hugging.

One Christmas Day, we youngsters organised a ping-pong knockout tournament on the kitchen table at Northcote Road, with a solemn, formal draw, using my dad's cap, which produced such classic first round ties as Auntie Alice vs Our Jimmy and Grandma vs Uncle George. At full extension, our playing surface measured a mere five foot by three, which called for a special technique, and even the most skilful player could be deceived by the gaps between the three sections of the table, which could deviate the ball unexpectedly in any direction, rather like the Lord's ridge.

I never had better times than these.

Alice v Annie, spectators from left Jim, Don, Mum, Ron

The Pantomime was, as now, always a Christmas affair, looked forward to with breathless anticipation by us children. In Sheffield, there was the choice of two theatres, the Lyceum or the Empire. We always sat perched high in the gods, presumably because it was all we could afford, but distance did not diminish our delight. I remember an *Aladdin* that scared the living daylights out of me. I remember radio stars like Jewell and Warris, Frank Randle and Ken Platt, but my favourite was and remains a working-class Lancashire comedian called Albert Modley, who did a bus conductor act that brought the house down. In 1959, the house was literally brought down. The Empire, at least twice as big as the Lyceum[50], was demolished. A decade later the Lyceum was threatened with the same fate, was saved by local activists, but remained closed and mouldering for 20 years.

Not living in a Catholic country, we knew nothing of carnival and of the merry parades and celebrations in some parts of the world. For us, the business of Lent was no more than Shrove Tuesday, when we ate pancakes for tea, with whatever accompaniment you fancied – lemon juice and sugar, or treacle (our word for Tate & Lyle's golden syrup), or gravy, et cetera. Ash Wednesday was often celebrated by eating hash[51], probably owing to a misunderstanding due to Sheffield folk's tendency to be economical with their aspirates. I was not aware of anyone in our small church community giving up things for Lent – perhaps the abstainers just kept quiet about their self-denial - in any case there was not a great deal to give up. St Valentine's Day too may have been on the ecclesiastical calendar, but it was more honoured in the breach than in the observance. You would have been hard pressed to find a Valentine's card in Heeley.

Easter was always something of a mystery to me as a small boy. Easter Sunday School was always an especially solemn affair, with lots of long faces and mournful music. Even the Boys' Brigade silenced their drums when they slow-marched past the church, which I understood was be-

---

[50] *To the best of my knowledge the Empire Theatre seated 3,000.*

[51] *No, this was not cannabis. It was a kind of stew made of finely chopped potatoes and meat, usually corned beef, often fried up.*

cause Jesus had died.[52] Yet on the other hand, the school holidays had started, usually on Maundy Thursday at four o'clock (hurray!), there were two football matches over the Easter weekend, and for Easter Sunday breakfast we ate boiled eggs, which we painted with funny faces.[53]

This confusing clash of mourning and celebration was certainly a principal reason why Good Friday, 1950, is one of the most memorable days of my childhood. We had broken up at the Annexe for the holidays and were in high spirits, as are all little boys at the start of school holidays. My pal Miffer told me that a group of J4 lads were meeting on Good Friday afternoon for a game of football on Fitzroy Road. Did I want to join in? I did, of course. I knew all the J4 lads and some of them were good players. Roy Silk, who lived in the posh houses down Northcote Road, was particularly good, and Kenneth Swift and Graham Nutt weren't bad. There were about a dozen of us, including a couple of lads from Ann's Road school that I didn't know. It was a great game, played on the street cobbles, with the church gate as one goal and the entrance to the gennel as the other. Beyond the gennel, Fitzroy Road led down to a select semicircle of posh houses, in a cul-de-sac. We didn't like the ball to go down towards these houses, as the residents were the sort of people who might complain, confiscate our ball, or even call the police. If the ball did run down into the cul-de-sac we agreed to regard it as out of play.

I should mention at this point that playing football in the street was strictly illegal, although, like Valentine's Day, this law was more honoured in the breach than in the observance, by small boys at least. It was very safe, and there were never any cars on Fitzroy Road. I knew that it was illegal, however, as my dad had told me stories of the times when he was 'pinched' by the bobby for playing football in the street. In our game, as twilight was drawing in, and I imagine that the score was around 20 all, the ball did in-

---

[52] *It is worth remarking that in those days it was customary for people to stand still and bow heads when a funeral cortege passed them in the street. Men removed their flat caps.*

[53] *We didn't have chocolate eggs and I don't remember chocolate featuring at all.*

deed once more run down into the cul-de-sac, and I was sent to fetch it. I did so in trepidation, as I knew that Vicky Cross's dad, who was a police inspector, lived down there and might be lying in wait to arrest me. My worst fears were realised. There he was, our ball at his feet, pencil and notebook in his hand. He told me I was breaking the law, on Good Friday of all days, I was old enough to know better and should be ashamed. He took down my name and address and cautioned me that a bobby would be coming to my house to see my parents. Who was I playing with? I told him some lads from school. He walked up to the other lads and took their names and addresses as well. It was very, very frightening.

The game broke up and we dispersed with our tails between our legs. I arrived home chastened. I hadn't told my mum that I would be playing football, as I knew she would have told me I couldn't, because it was Good Friday and also illegal. Not only was I scared of getting a cop-it from my parents, but I was also afflicted with guilt at having played football on the day when Jesus was dying on the cross. I was also anxious about having to go to court and answer to a judge for my crime. Mum took the attitude of let-that-be-a-lesson-to-me, but when Dad came home from work, I had the feeling that he found my arrest quite amusing, and I think I caught sight of Mum stifling a giggle. If I hadn't known better, I might have suspected Dad was quite proud of me. For a few weeks, I remained in fear and trembling about the impending visit of the bobby and further action by the law, but there was no dread knock on the front door, and I was not summonsed. I presume that the Home Secretary had decided to take no further action.

Whitsuntide was, and is, a religious festival taking place exactly seven weeks after Easter, celebrating the descent of the Holy Spirit to the Disciples. The Whitsuntide holiday, like Easter a movable feast, could fall between early May and mid-June, and has now been replaced by the official Spring Bank Holiday. Whit Monday was the day of church parades. Around nine-thirty on Whit Monday morning, the Boys Brigade assembled on Northcote Road outside the church hall, in smartest drill uniform, along with the Sunday School children and any other member of the church congregation who wish to join them, for the parade to

Meersbrook Park. Leading the parade was the church banner, borne proudly aloft by two unfortunate and preferably burly members of the church or Boys Brigade. Once only, at my suggestion, my dad carried the banner, on one of his very few holiday days, and so maybe reluctantly, although he did not complain. At ten o'clock we began to wind painfully slowly through the streets of Heeley and Meersbrook to meet up with similar parades from all the nonconformist churches in the area, all the time serenaded by the Boys Brigade marching band, in which I was a drummer and Miffer was a bugler[54]. We were greeted down every street by crowds lining the pavements, exactly like homecoming Cup Final winners. The nearer we came to the park, the denser the crowds. Finally, all the church parades, converged into one, a brilliant feat of organisation marshalled by I know not whom, perhaps by sheer luck, or by goodwill to all men, or even the police. I don't remember. It was a strange madness scarcely understandable in today's climate, but it did happen. The parade from Northcote Road to Meersbrook Park took almost two hours and the crowds in the park were vast. The parade members were set free to join their families and join in or listen to the hymn singing. And that was that. Nothing else. It always felt to me an anti-climax. And a relief. Then the parades reassembled and marched back home to their churches, on a more direct, non-stop route this time.

Prior to my years in the Boys Brigade, I knew Whitsuntide as the time when we children all had new clothes, which we showed off proudly to our friends and relatives on the Whit Sunday circuit, receiving sixpences in reward for donning and displaying our splendid outfits. One year, 1949 or 1950, all the boy cousins, David, Bobby, Jimmy, Geoff and I, were wearing identical new caps, a superb blue and red number, bought independently by the three sisters and so coincidentally identical, all from t' Stores on Ecclesall Road. I presume they were a special offer or just the cheapest. These matching caps were the source of some hilarity

---

[54] *Ray Smith (Miffer) and I were in the Boys Brigade band from 1953-58.*

Whitsuntide Parade 1958, me leading the band on the side-drum

amongst the adults. Uncle Don especially made quite a few jokes in his customary slow, acerbic style of witticism. There we sat in the park on Whit Monday morning, looking for all the world like a school trip. A posh elderly lady passing by remarked how smart we all looked, and did we all go to the same prep school? My mum replied yes, Borstal. The mouth of the distinguished grey-haired one fell open in dismay. It seemed that she had not developed as refined a sense of irony as Mum.

As I have mentioned the Boys Brigade, I should comment briefly in the large part it played in the leisure and social life of my teens. I joined the Cubs as a small boy, equipped with cap, badge, neckerchief and woggle, hated it for its mind-numbing dullness, was awarded my tenderfoot, whatever that may have signified, but then decided the whole business was not for me. I joined the Life Boys, the junior Boys Brigade, which turned out to be more fun and games. It had frog football and leapfrog for a start, and it was right there on Northcote Road. The BB was a bit like school, a bit like the army, a bit like Sunday School, but had games too. We learned first aid, we learned to tie knots and other worthy skills, we passed tests and earned badges, we played games and sport, we drilled like real soldiers and sometimes we marched, but unlike the real army we didn't kill anybody. We also did a little heads-bowed praying, and there was Sunday morning Bible Class, a sort of mini church service in a tiny room. I went along with all this, never missing a day. I must have liked it, or at least respected it, rated it, or perhaps I was just loyal. Loyalty seemed to me to be life's key virtue, in books and films, in sport, in family, in friendships.

Genuinely good people ran the Boys Brigade company, none of them seeking personal glory or advancement. So, thanks to you Charlie Finch, to you Jack Briggs, to you Donald Bell, to you Donald Hibbert, for all the love, all the fun, and I know it's not fashionable, for all the benevolent discipline too.

Christian religion was at the heart of the Boys Brigade, as it was in most aspects of my childhood and adolescence. It was a kind of club to which you had automatic membership, and I was a loyal member. In my teens I began to question the vague concept of heaven that was promised to the faithful. Did other people really believe it? I was sure that Charlie Finch did. He was so patently as straight as a die. Young Donald Bell also was 100% a believer. The goodness oozed out of his very pores. I remember that he spoke of kneeling to pray at lights out in the barracks, amid all those rough National Service squaddies. I could not imagine an unworthy thought ever crossing his mind. Jack Briggs was an intellectual type and said little about Jesus, and Donald Hibberd gave off a 'bit-of-a-lad' aura, and so I wasn't certain about the two of them. So, back to heaven, did I qualify for entry? On balance, I thought not, as I certainly was not perfect, but I did know a lot of people who were more sinful than I was. Perhaps I would merely be given a stern ticking off by St Peter and placed in an Improvers Section of Heaven. Surely I would not be flung into the fiery furnace, for God was all-forgiving, I had heard. I discounted the vengeful Old Testament God, as He was just for the Israelites, and in the Olden Days anyway. I didn't feel I could discuss the matter with anyone, mainly out of embarrassment but also for fear of being considered a backslider and not sound. Eventually I decided that death and heaven were a long way into the future and to go with the flow for the time being, as a kind of insurance policy. I would decide later, when I had more evidence. Quite a mature decision in retrospect.

There was, however, one dangerous incident at the City Hall. Billy Graham was in London preaching to the masses, and Ray and I decided to go together to hear the relayed address at the City Hall. We were 14 or 15.

The hall was packed to the rafters and there was a weird electricity in the air. There was comforting music playing as we waited for Graham to begin. I have since seen and heard speeches to the masses by Adolf Hitler, but Billy Graham was no less compelling, even from 150 miles away and invisible. I remember nothing of what he said, but I do remember the people streaming towards the stage afterwards, under the pressure of constantly repeated imprecations by the Great Man, first in a trickle, then in their dozens, then their scores, then their hundreds to commit themselves to the Billy Graham Crusade, to promise their futures to the great cause, and to Jesus too, although the latter part was less clear.

I felt an unbearably powerful magnetic force pulling me towards the stage to join the host of believers, and I was only saved by my God-given reticence, my instinct not to make a fuss or to show myself up. For once it was a shortcoming that served me well. As Ray said afterwards, when we had escaped into the cool, sane air of Barker's Pool, "I was watching you. If you'd blinked and stood up, I'd have been a goner!" I confessed to him that I had felt exactly the same way.

It was around this time that St Peter's acquired a vicar, or perhaps minister is the correct term. The church had never had a vicar before, at least as far as Mum remembered, and so this was a great novelty, and I felt it gave St Peter's a new, enhanced status. I had first spotted the Reverend Brierley one Sunday morning, as I emerged from the belfry after my bell-ringing duties (I was paid a small quarterly fee for ringing the church bell each Sunday morning and evening). I assumed him to be a visiting preacher, but he was permanent, well, temporarily permanent.

Brierley certainly livened up proceedings with his white vestments and his hypnotic Irish brogue. Where he had come from and what were the circumstances of his appointment were a mystery, to me at least, and no-one else seemed to be much wiser. We presumed he had been appointed by Charlie Finch and the old ladies, the church's elders. I did wonder how we could afford to pay him.

Our new vicar had the gift of the blarney, a charming manner and the aura of a good shepherd. He brought a new spice to church services, and even some of us teenagers went along to check him out. At least it was somewhere to be on a Sunday night, and indoors too. Sylvia put on her smart dress and makeup and came with me, which was a bonus, as she held my hand affectionately. The Reverend Brierley was considered by all to be a Good Thing, even though he wasn't from Heeley.

About eighteen months later, Mum opened the News of the World to find pictures of a furtive-looking Brierley and a full-page article denouncing him as a bigamist (or trigamist) and a fraud. Nothing was said at St Peter's, no official announcement was made. There was, disappointingly, no public defrocking of the Reverend Brierley. He merely vanished as suddenly as he had arrived. Charlie and the elders, and the rest of us for that matter, carried on in tight-lipped silence, in our restored minister-free state, although there was a little whispering in the pews.

Whilst I am on the subject of religion, which I seem to be, perhaps a brief word on how I felt about other religions would throw some light on post-war British society. Well, Heeley society at least. I think I can best sum up my attitude as benevolent disdain. It was a given that other religions were misguided or plain wrong and were practised only by benighted foreigners. I was confident that Gladys Aylward and co would set them all on the straight and narrow eventually, and, in the meantime, God might well be understanding about their lack of opportunity to find the strait gate. I knew little of other religions. For me Islam meant the Saracen enemies of the excellent Richard the Lionheart, Buddhists were fat, silent and peaceable, and Hindus were thin and poor. I didn't even know any Catholics or Jews. Ethnic minorities were also absent from my life. There was Roy Chan in the year above me at the Annexe, who Miffer said had Chinese parents, but he was normal apart from the shape of his face, and there was a small dark-skinned old man who lived on Northcote Road, whom everyone called "t' darkie", but apart from that my world was monochrome, except when I went to the pictures. Even at University, I don't remember crossing paths with any people of colour, except perhaps for the odd glimpse of a Persian girl, about whom the received view was that she was rich and aloof. Ignorance was bliss, I suppose. I was certainly ignorant, but in mitigation my world was small and my horizon narrow.

It is time to remind myself of the title of this chapter and of fun times. The premier fun time of the year, the time looked forward to even more ardently than Christmas, was without doubt the annual summer holiday. I imagine Dad looked forward to this two-week oasis in his long year of work even more keenly than I did. Dad's annual holiday allocation amounted to Easter Monday, Whit Monday, two weeks in the summer, Christmas Day, and Boxing Day. For him New Year's Day was a working day like any other. Consequently, when he was finally on holiday at the seaside, he was up with the proverbial lark at 5 am, down at the harbour with the fishermen, sipping a cup of tea and reading the ink off the newspaper, to squeeze every last drop of enjoyment out of his unaccustomed freedom.

For all the years of my childhood and teens the two week summer holiday was at the seaside, usually Bridlington, and always half-board in a boarding house, if possible with a landlady recommended by a friend or relative. Mum was very much the Chancellor of our Exchequer and somehow saved up enough for the summer holiday. I have no idea where she kept the money, filtered out of dad's weekly wage packet, perhaps in a jar under the bed, perhaps in a secret drawer. In the spring and early summer, she and Auntie Annie always took on seasonal casual work, which involved giggling and eating strawberries at the jam factory at the bottom of the Cutting (which was the name everyone gave to Carrfield Road), perhaps earning as much as five pounds per week to supplement the summer holiday fund.

In my memory, these two weeks in Bridlington were one long festival of sunshine, breeze, beach, sand-castles, deck-chairs, donkey rides, swing-boats, cricket, and swimming in the North Sea until I was blue with cold. Cousin Geoff was always present, as were sometimes David, Robert and Jimmy, although their dad often had different holiday weeks. The holiday began on the last Saturday in July with the bus down to the town centre with our cardboard suitcases, to join the frighteningly long queue in Union Street for the Sheffield United Tours charas[55] to Bridlington. It seemed like the whole of Sheffield was decamping en masse to Brid, which in those days was a clean and wholesome resort and gave good value for money. There were rainy days, of course, but then at least Geoff and I were allowed to buy a comic, for him the *Dandy* or *Beano*, for me a Superman or Captain Marvel comic. These we would read over and over in our boarding house bedroom. And there was always the amusement arcade, with the wonderful slot machines, which sometimes even allowed you to win.

---

[55] *We called coaches charas (pronounced shara) or charabangs, a relic of the old word char-a-banc, a horse drawn vehicle or an early motor-coach, with benches in rows for its passengers. I still use the word, ironically.*

1946

1948

1951

1950 Me as teapot, Geoff as cowboy, David (centre) as (??)

1951 Mum, me, David

1952

One year, probably 1951, for a change, we tried Yarmouth, but this proved to be a big disappointment and the journey there seemed to take for ever. I for one longed for the familiar scenes of our own Yorkshire coast. The following year, I was sent on holiday with Auntie Annie and Uncle Ron, sharing a single bed with Geoffrey. I assume now it was because my parents couldn't afford to go away that summer.

Then, in 1953, Auntie Alice and Uncle George discovered the WTA, The Workers' Travel Association, and its holiday home in Highcliffe on Sea in Hampshire. Beacon Lodge was a grand, white-painted country club converted into a budget hotel for the WTA, which Auntie Alice pronounced dobble-you-tee-ay, to the amusement and mockery of her sisters.

Beacon Lodge, situated up a long gravel driveway, on a clifftop with exquisite sea-views, had extensive grounds, including a beautiful front lawn with an immaculate putting green and steps down to the beach. It was surrounded on both sides by woodland. It had outbuildings such as a snooker room with a full-sized table, a games room with table tennis, darts, bar skittles and shove-ha'penny sets. For a boy like me, sport-loving and competitive, it was the very heaven. I was allowed to play snooker and billiards on an unbearably professional table, twelve foot long and six foot wide, for heaven's sake! At the front of the property there was a sports field with tennis courts and a croquet lawn.

Not only were there all these games facilities, but the host organised weekly competitions in all the sports and games. I enrolled in every competition and persuaded Mum and Dad to join in several also. This meant seeking out the opponent drawn against you in, say, Round One of the shove-ha'penny or Round Two of the snooker. It was an all-consuming programme of competitive fixtures for me, such that I had little time left over even for beach activities. The meals were not excellent, leading to the odd grumble from the adults, but I had no complaints. This was a dream holiday. In the evenings, things just got better and better. The host always put on a full evening's entertainment in the ballroom, admittedly including some dancing for the oldies, but also competitions and team-games with prizes. There were also new and fascinating voices and accents, from the South of England.

Above, Dad at Beacon Lodge, 1954

One evening, my sentimental education was initiated when I was propositioned by an older woman, from London no less. It was my first taste of the sleazy side of teenage life. I was 13, and an older girl called Valerie, who was 14 or 15 and had a pronounced bosom, came to me during one of these social evenings and invited me to go for a walk with her. 'You've clicked there, lad', commented our new friend Mr Copestake from Clitheroe, with a wink and a grin. Mum and Dad said nothing. Valerie led me by the hand in silence down the main drive and then, when we reached the anonymity of darkness, pulled me into the bushes, where she put her arms around my neck and kissed me long and hard for at least a minute. I did my best to join in and held her imprisoned in a vice-like grip for a few seconds after the kiss, until she shrugged me off and said 'Let's go back now'. Was that it? I wondered. So that was what they did. She seemed contented enough with the 'walk'. On balance, I still preferred snooker.

We repeated the idyllic Highcliffe holiday the following summer, 1954, and then, in 1955, cousin David and I were inexplicably sent off together unaccompanied for his first and my third dose of this Beacon Lodge bliss. I have never quite understood why. We were both still only 15, although David had now left school to start work at the Midland Bank. Perhaps it was a sort of rite of passage for him, and I was sent along for company? I shall never know.

One summer event worth recording, if only for the fact that it was a complete washout, was my brainwave of organising a family trip to the seaside to celebrate the coronation of the Queen. Being just as ardent a royalist as everyone else in 1953, I was eager to mark the Great Day in our own special way. Mum agreed, and the idea met with general family approval, except in the case of cousin June who had already booked a seat for the event in front of a friend's nine-inch television.

I collected weekly contributions from all branches of the family and recorded them in a vocabulary book. I kept the cash in a biscuit tin. Mum booked a bus big enough for our family of 18. On Coronation Day, we set off at 8 am for Cleethorpes.

It rained hard every minute of the day. Cleethorpes was deserted. Even the amusement arcades were closed, as were most cafés. I spent most of the day with cousin David, in a bus shelter on the Prom.

At three o'clock we set off back home, defeated by the foul weather. We had spent the whole day insulated from news of the rest of the world. The Coronation had passed us by without even a glance in our direction. I suspect that, even the best part of seven decades later, the Queen still knows nothing of our special contribution to her special day.

Bonfire Night, Guy Fawkes Night, or Fireworks Night stood out like a fiery beacon to compensate us for the dark, damp and gloomy autumn days of November and December[56]. We youngsters looked forward to it for weeks. In the week before November 5th, we gathered branches, twigs, scrap wood and anything combustible to build the bonfire. Ours was always built at the bottom of Mrs Woodhouse's part of the yard, which was sheltered on three sides by brick walls and ideal for a cosy camp-fire style evening for everyone in the yard. There was always bonfire toffee, parkin, and toffee apples; chestnuts and potatoes were roasted (often incinerated and inedible) in the bonfire. Some lads made Guy Fawkes effigies out of discarded clothes stuffed with straw or rags, and the more enterprising set up in business at street corners begging for 'a penny for the guy'. I went as far as making a guy once or twice, and we burned him ritually on top our bonfire, for the sake of authenticity, but I didn't have the chutzpah to do the penny-for-the-guy-please-gov'nor bit.

There were fireworks too, bought from Woolhouses' newsagents, of course. Golden rod, silver rain, bangers, and rockets, which we fired off from milk bottles. My favourite was naturally the jumping crackers, which exploded five or six times, and leapt about in random directions, scaring the unwary. Some bad lads would put bangers in empty metal dustbins to make a frightening boom. Not I. I was too much of a goody-goody.

---

[56] *Hallowe'en was not celebrated in my world. I don't think I had even heard of it.*

Even though I acknowledge that what we were doing was symbolically burning Catholic dissenters, and that it would be far from PC or woke to perpetuate this heinous ritual, I miss those November 5^{ths} so very much whenever the damp, dreary autumn comes around once again.

XI Grandma and dialect

I have mentioned my grandmother a number of times in previous chapters, but she merits a short extra section devoted to her, not only because she was the only grandparent I knew well, but also because she is my direct line to the local dialect of my ancestors.

As a youngster, it was a bit of a mystery to me how Grandma's name was Price, as I knew that my mother's maiden name was Billard, but I puzzled it out eventually! She had an elementary education, possibly until the age of 11, and had basic literacy and numeracy skills, but I am not sure that she read much beyond *Woman's Own* or *The Star,* and she certainly never read me any stories. She was numerate enough to work out sums like one and eleven-pence three farthings plus eighteen and fourpence halfpenny. Very few of us were not, as a result of having to deal with a currency which included farthings, ha'pennies, pennies, threepenny bits of silver and bronze, sixpences, shillings, florins, half-crowns, ten-bob notes and occasionally guineas, and demanded manipulation of multiples of four, twelve, twenty and occasionally twenty-one. Grandma was also competent at dealing with stones, pounds, ounces, feet and inches, which required reckoning in multiples of 14, 16 and 12. This is not to mention the inconvenient way that a mile was composed of 1760 yards, or 5280 feet, or eight furlongs, each of 220 yards, or ten chains, (or was it bushels and pecks?) and that the freezing point of water was a ludicrous 32 degrees.

I suspect that there had been little peace in Grandma's life, and I remember her as permanently anxious and agitated, with trembling hands and little patience. On the other hand, there was never one second's doubt that she cared for us grandchilder[57] all very dearly. I remember her taking Geoff and me on a chara trip to the coast, Skegness or Mablethorpe, near the end of her life, and returning limping painfully and completely exhausted in exchange for her kind efforts. To our shame we made fun of her limp.

I knew her only as a white-haired old lady, who was always short of breath and suffered from severe asthma, always carrying her atomiser with her. She also frequently needed, in desperation, to burn Potter's Asthma Remedy[58] in a tin lid to help her breathing, a process which created a hateful, acrid smell. She and Mum were very close, and Mum was always on hand to care for her, as she lived nearby. In fact, she very often spent the evening in our kitchen, playing knockout whist, rummy and canasta, or listening to *Itma*, Valentine Dyall's creepy *Man in Black*, or the unctuous Donald Peers perpetually crooning *By a Babbling Brook*.

Grandma died in hospital when I was around eleven, and even at that age I realised that her dying was not all bad, as at least she was released from the unrelenting struggle to breathe and the distressing pain in her limbs.

One of the most fascinating things about Grandma was her language, which was a far cry from the lingua franca of King Edward's, but none the less worthy for that. She loved *Mrs Dale's Diary*, but I can't for the life of me think why, as the excruciating cut-glass accent of the actors, leavened by a dose of mockney from the charlady, was light years away from any voices relevant to her life. I can only imagine that she regarded it as some fantasy world where people were so prosperous that even doctor's wives were constantly complaining about being hard up and wondering where the next Axminster carpet was coming from. In September 2021, I listened to an edition of Mrs Dale's Diary, rehashed on Ra-

---

[57] *The traditional plurals* childer *and* grandchilder *were what Grandma used.*

[58] *It has since been demonstrated that Potter's Asthma Remedy, far from being beneficial, was actual the cause of emphysema.*

dio 4 Extra, and found it atrocious in so many ways, but above all riddled with snobbery. It would certainly have confirmed Grandma's position on the social ladder – just below the bottom rung.

Grandma's Sheffield English was not archaic in terms of local dialect, but she did have a few words and expressions which were peculiar to her and no doubt historic. Whenever we children asked what was for tea, she always, always replied with the same formula: "Lay-oes 'o' meddlers and crusses for young ducks", which meant [something nasty] for meddlers, and crusts for good children. She often described children as being 'like clamvecherous thieves', when they were clamouring round her for food, or when they had polished off a plate of bread and jam in double-quick time: 'there weren't a skerrick[59] left!' When a grandchild was buzzing round like a dervish, she would say 'he's like a scopperdiddle'. These are beautifully onomatopoeic sayings and I have found references to a couple of them on the local forum website[60], with various stabs at explaining what a scopperdiddle is, including a flying shuttle on a weaving loom, a toy clown that ran up and down a stick, a mouse, a rascal, a crayfish, and a small spinning top. I believe this last explanation is correct. I found an entry in the complete Oxford Dictionary, 1989 edition, which looks like the same word: scopperil (or scopperelle), 'a small spinning top spun between thumb and finger', [a term that is] 'often applied to an active restless child, or a squirrel'. Perhaps I should write and tell the lexicographers how to spell it properly.

As to clamvecherous, I surmise that it was connected to clammed or clemmed, which in Sheffield meant very hungry. Confusingly, clammed/clemmed also meant very cold! Similarly, 'starving' also had this hungry/cold double meaning. Continuing with the food theme, if you 'golloped'[61] your tea you were a 'gobblety-guts, and if you put too much jam or butter on your bread you were told to 'gi' o'er[62] larraping

---

[59] *skerrick* – *a tiny bit, scrap, usually used in the negative 'not a skerrick'.*
[60] www.sheffieldforum.co.uk
[61] *gollop = eat greedily or too quickly.*
[62] *gi' o'er (give over) = stop*

it on', but these were expressions used commonly by others also.

Grandma was a frequent user of the special vocabulary some adults use when addressing small children; head was 'polly', hands were 'dannies', eggs were 'chucky-eggs' (usually soft-boiled), sheep, cows and horses were 'baa-lambs, moo-cows and poppoes' respectively, and lights were lilliloes (lily-loes?). She was constantly worried that we would get in trouble; 'tha maun't do that', to which the correct response was 'Oh no, Grandma, I dursn't[63] do that, I'd get a cop-it from me Dad'. She chided us for 'mithering' her, getting under her feet, and for our 'loppy' (filthy) hands, knees, face and neck which made us 'look like chimbly-sweeps'. To be fair to us, it was Sheffield that was loppy; the air pollution in the 1940s and 1950s, due to emissions from factories and the ubiquitous domestic coal fires, was so bad that a shirt collar (and children's hands and necks!) turned black in half a day, and smogs were endemic in autumn and winter. She (and Mum for that matter) were also forever spoiling my fun by telling me to 'gi' o'er scraumin'[64] all o'er t' furniture', which apparently I did quite a lot. Another bad habit we children were often accused of was teeming and ladling, pouring things from one cup to another, which of course children love to do. "Gi' o'er teemin' an' ladlin'! "

Another Grandma special was her frequent complaint about having to traipass around – 'They hadn't got it in at Boots's, so I've had to traipass around town all afternoon for it'. I knew what traipass around meant but had only heard Heeley people use the expression. It was only when I read more widely that I discovered that there actually was a 'real' word traipse, which meant exactly the same. A revelation! I suppose, looking back, traipsing around was a trial for Grandma, with her dreadful asthma.

One last saying of Grandma's that I must mention is her expression "fast brazen 'ussy", meaning a naughty lass but also with tinge of loose morals. I try to perpetuate this gorgeous phrase, in fun, whenever I have the opportunity, but people just 'look at me gone out' when they hear it. We boys

---

[63] *maun't or mon't = mustn't; dursn't = daren't*
[64] *scrauming = a cross between crawling and climbing*

could be 'fast brazent' too, of course, but this just meant cheeky, with no hint of moral turpitude.

Moving away from Grandma as an exemplar, a few other expressions stand out as of their time. If, as a child, I was not approaching a task competently, or not holding a tool properly, or generally being a bit 'cack-handed', Dad or an uncle would say 'Nay, son, th'art not framing, tha pie-can[65]', Mum would say 'frame, lad!' and when I got it right 'now you're framing a bit'. If Geoffrey and I were in a particularly friendly phase, people would say we were like Tib and Lal – I have no idea who Tib and Lal were.

A 'bonny woman' was not pretty in Sheffield but plump and big-busted. Bonny was not used to describe a baby (pronounced babby in Sheffield). A 'brussen' lad who was always 'braunging' was a stocky lad who was always boasting. 'Skinny' meant miserly, and 'dead spozzy' was very lucky. If it was 'siling down' it was heavier rain than when it was merely 'chucking it down'. 'It's black o'er Bill's mother's' meant 'look at those black clouds over there, it will rain soon'. We didn't say 'yes'; instead we said 'aye', although 'dead common' people said 'ah'. If my mother had heard me say 'ah' instead of 'yes' she would have 'played merry hell (or allelujah) with me'.

If meat was overcooked, it was 'crozzled' ('I like me bacon a bit crozzled'), if it was of poor quality it was 'rammy', as was anything else declared to be 'rammy' or 'dead rammy', and 'rammel' was odds and ends of no value – 'mek sure tha teks all thi rammel 'oo-om wi' thee'[66]. Another word for bits and bobs and maybe also a surfeit of ornaments or trinkets on a mantlepiece was 'tranklements'. If adults were ill, they were 'badly', but childer were just poorly. People could just be feeling 'a bit off o' t' ooks'[67] or 'a bit maungy', although maungy was more often used to describe a dog or cat that had a patchy coat. If you were dozy or slow you were called 'datal', presumably from the theory that employees on piecework were a lot quicker than those on a daily rate.

---

[65] *pie-can = a lovely, gentle rebuke to a child = you're a twerp (but I love you), rather like the more recent 'What are you like?'*
[66] *make sure you take all your rubbish home with you*
[67] *= a bit off the hooks = a trifle unwell, not quite oneself.*

Sport and games had a few idiosyncratic words. In football, if you didn't relish the physical aspect of the game, you were accused of 'neshing your tackles'; you were 'nesh' if you were scared of the cold or felt the cold and were considered a bit of a softy. The word nesh is still current in both senses. If a player 'cabbaged' at a throw-in or free kick, he was stealing a few yards; similarly, you were 'cabbaging' if you stood too close in darts, et cetera. 'He's cabbaging, referee!' Goal posts were goal 'stoops', and football shorts were football knickers. In cricket a left-handed batsman was a 'dolly-posh'. In table games and in a queue, kale meant turn: 'It's thy kale', or 'tha's missed thi kale'.

Mum was constantly trying to raise her and my standard of speech from what she considered common speech, or slovenly speech, and was proficient at aspirates without sounding too posh, but Dad and Grandma were incorrigible dialect speakers. The result was that I became pretty much trilingual, fluent in both local dialect and King Ted's English, as well as Mum's in-between version.

XII Holiday jobs

From the age of sixteen, I decided it was time to 'pay my way' a little by getting a summer job. Most lads at school went looking for office jobs or worked for their Dad's firm in collar and tie. No such 'bobby's job'[68] for me! I was determined to show my working-class credentials and prove that I was not a softy just because I had stayed on in the sixth form. Perhaps I wanted to affirm the dignity of manual labour and show solidarity with my social class?
☺ ☺ ☺ Yes, that was probably it.

Quite a number of my Annexe classmates had been in full-time work for a year by now and were bringing home enviable pay-packets, as milkmen, window-cleaners, parks gardeners, or apprentice chippies. I had done what I had always done, stayed in the groove and done what people expected of me, passed my scholarship, gone to grammar school, done my O Levels, with university beckoning around the next corner.

My first job was for a month or so at Black's woodyard on Queen's Road. I can only guess that the boss must have been either a philanthrope or in a good mood, when I turned up begging for gainful employment, as I must have presented a poor wee timorous beastie of a figure, at my eight stone

---

[68] A 'bobby's job' was one that involved no hard (physical) work and still paid pretty well – 'That's a reight bobby's job he's got!'

wet through, or as Grandma would have said more imaginatively, 'a yard of pump-water stretched out'.

When I arrived on the first day of my employment, they seemed to have forgotten I was coming and the boss was on holiday. Eventually, after a lot of head-scratching from the deputy boss, I was assigned to the warehouse, where I did not receive a euphoric welcome from the warehouseman, who was used to a quiet, solitary life in his basement room, reading the paper. 'What am I supposed to do wi' 'im?' Realising that his cup of joy ranneth not over at the prospect of me under his feet all the time, I tried to be on my best behaviour and as helpful as a useless teenager like me could be. I did graduate to handling some long, heavy planks by the end of my stint, in a Laurel and Hardy sort of way and at great risk to windows and other woodyard personnel, but the warehouseman and I did not get on well, and he was glad to see the back of me. I departed, to his delight, after four weeks, leaving scarcely a ripple in the smooth running of Black's woodyard.

My last summer job of all, six years later in the Whitbread's depot on Chesterfield Road, was equally uneventful, perhaps because I already had some experience of handling beer. Our job was to load, unload and stack various sizes of barrel, whenever a 'waggin' or a 'Scammell' arrived[69]. At slack times, the lads would beg the foreman to 'oppen a pin, gaffer' and we would spend a pleasant social hour or two drinking its contents, about 32 pints, and playing snooker. It was congenial work, I shall not deny, if a little tough on the waistline.

In all I had completed seven summers of holiday jobs before permanent employment in my first teaching post. Two of the summers were with the Sheffield City Engineers, the Council road-menders, two summers in the trenches with pick and shovel. I worked with rough lads with hard hands and big biceps. Unlike the modern softies, we wore no gloves or helmets. On warm days we were naked from the waist up, sweaty and filthy. I was fairly useless in the trenches, and it was a blessing that I was not around for World War I.

---

[69] *The lads at the depot called a lorry a 'waggin' and an articulated lorry a Scammell.*

However murderously I swung it, my pick seemed cursed to hit nothing but stubborn stones. Nevertheless, I worked hard, did Saturday morning overtime, built up new muscles, calloused hands and a first-rate suntan, and brought home a weekly wage packet as big as Dad's.

My first two weeks with the City Engineers involved laying new pavement flagstones. I had been warned about useless young apprentices being sent off for a long weight or a long stand, a spirit level bubble, a left-handed screwdriver, sky hooks, et cetera, and so I immediately rumbled my flag-laying mentor when he told me: 'This is buggered, goo and get me a beetle out o' t' jungle, lad.' A beetle out of the jungle, eh? I was onto his little japes and told him so. It turned out that the request was genuine - a beetle is a wooden mallet for knocking flagstones into place, and the jungle was what the workers called their cabin. My face was red.

Next it was off to another site for my gang, and there into the trenches. The chief old lag of the trenches was a ruddy faced-fellow in his forties, who was an accomplished yarn-spinner, his tales often involving the bedroom exploits of him and 't' owd lass', with lascivious details which were shocking to my young ears. A sort of leader of the gang, he had a few watchwords. Whenever it started to rain, he would say to our emphysematous old foreman: 'Raining, Arthur, how are we off for t' jungle?' I spent a number of rainy summer afternoons playing cards with the lads in the jungle and praying for it not to clear up before home time. Another of his sayings was an always theatrically delivered "On the wire", which meant that a boss from the office was arriving in a van to check on our progress, but my favourite was reserved for Friday afternoons:

"'E's 'ere, I Presume".
"Who's I Presume?" I enquired the first time I heard him say it.
"I Presume. Tha knows, I presume you lot want to work o' Sat'day mornin'."

It was a correct presumption by I Presume; Saturday morning work was paid at time and a half rate!

The second summer that I worked for the City Engineers followed a different pattern. I was switched weekly between various gangs as a supplementary labourer on highway projects, which made it difficult to form any relationships, get to know fellow workers and be accepted. There was the usual excavating of trenches and digging up and replacing cracked and broken paving stones, until I was dispatched to the new Parkway construction to help pour concrete into the central barrier, a noisy, dirty and unpleasant job involving guiding ton after ton of relentlessly flowing concrete down a long chute into a mould. It was chain-gang labour, and I was pleased to be transferred from that site.

For the last two weeks of my summer employment, I was assigned to St Mary's Church on Bramall Lane. This was work of an unexpected kind. I arrived to find the whole of the northern side of the church grounds protected from public view by high blue canvas screens. The foreman was waiting for me and explained that we would be 'digging up t' bodies in t' graveyard' for a road widening scheme to turn St Mary's Gate into a dual carriageway. It was gruesome work, slow and painstaking when we hit upon rotting coffins, which we had to pick out fragment by fragment, to avoid further damage to the mouldering bones. Occasionally we found a complete skeleton, once of an infant, and even a wedding ring or two. There were a few family vaults, which only the foreman was allowed to enter. The graves, we were assured, were all very old, the bodies buried at least a hundred, even two hundred years ago. The remains were to be re-buried together at Abbey Lane cemetery, with due decency was the claim.

I became used to the eerie, Burke and Hare nature of the work and blasé about raising the corpses, but the special smell which assailed us when standing deep in a grave was such an emetic that I could never eat my packed lunch and eventually stopped bothering to bring one. When my summer stint ended, although I missed the craic and the excitement at what we might find six or more feet down in the earth, I was relieved that it was over.

Every December from the age of 18 [70], for the ten days or so between end of the University autumn term and Christmas, I worked for the GPO as a temporary postman. We

---

[70] *You had to be 18 to work as a postman.*

clocked in around 6 am, were given an armband and a sack of sorted mail to deliver, and sent off on the bus to our round, while the regular postman stayed back in the sorting office. I always did at least three rounds per day, and we could stay out delivering for as long as we wanted before we clocked off. The number of Christmas cards and packages sent through the post was colossal and there were always plenty to deliver. Even if it rained or snowed, being a relief postman was good work for a fit young man. We worked all the way through until lunchtime on Christmas Day – it was double time on Christmas Day!

One year I worked nights in the parcels sorting office on Edmund Road. This was virtually a bobby's job. A lot of the work consisted in hurling parcels into various labelled compartments, a lot of it was just standing around waiting. I also had jolly trips out to Midland and Victoria stations in a parcels van to send sacks of Christmas presents on their way by British Rail. On Christmas Eve around midnight all the GPO staff (including me) decamped to a pub and spent a couple of hours drinking beer and smoking, behind closed doors. I thought this was a fine arrangement and lost any fear of being fired after the first pint.

The other strand of my summer job experience was at dairies. I spent much of one summer at the massive Sheffield and Ecclesall Co-op dairy in Archer Road. This was conveyor belt work and probably the hardest physical labour I have experienced. My mate was a phenomenally strong man, well over six foot tall with muscles on his muscles. I think the conveyor belt was tuned to his speed. Our work, in a cramped space, was to lift full crates of milk, 24 pints, off the belt and stack them behind us for a forklift truck to take away. If we didn't keep up with the belt, then crates of milk would crash off the end onto a concrete floor and smash. We started very early, at 3 am, six days a week. It was exhausting work. By late morning, if I was still standing, the work became easier, as we were now only lifting crates of empties to be taken off to be washed for the next day's supply.

Eventually, I was lucky enough to break my finger playing for the Imps, which meant I could report to the office and resign. Never in my life have I been so relieved to have an incapacitating injury.

I also spent two summers delivering milk for the Brightside and Carbrook Co-op dairy, in the industrial part of the city. The most surprising aspect of being a milkman in this north-eastern quarter of Sheffield was that it was a very dirty job. I would arrive home after a shift with my clothes and my face filthy and my hands and arms black. This whole area of the city was covered in a thick layer of soot and grime, and the air was extremely polluted. I wince to think of the state of our lungs.

For these milk rounds I was always paired with a regular milkman for a two-week stint, while his mate was on holiday. Mostly we delivered silver top, regular milk, but not homogenised like the universal product in our supermarkets today. There was also the so-called Guernsey milk, with a gold top, which had twice as much cream content and cost twopence a pint extra. Our customers left Co-op tokens ('milk checks') on the doorstep along with the empties. One or two characters that I worked with stand out in my memory, although none of them was a great conversationalist. Their priority was getting the round done as fast as possible, probably so that they could go back to bed, as being a milkman meant very early rising. In my case, living at the other side of the city, early rising meant 3.30 a.m., to catch the first bus into town.

One of my mates, let's call him Albert, used to turn up at work in an immaculate Bentley, which he parked in the dairy yard. I discovered that he was a bookie as well as a milkman, and that his round was the shortest of all so that he could finish around 11 o'clock and do his real work, unofficial and sub rosa, of course, as off-course betting was illegal. It suited me very well to finish at 11 o'clock. However, one snag with Albert's round was that it included the Blackburn Meadows sewage farm, and Albert chose this salubrious venue for our mid-round break and breakfast. By the end of my fortnight with Albert I was just beginning to become acclimatised to the stench. Albert was the most silent of men, although he did explain to me why there were so many tomato plants growing around the edges of the sewerage filtration tanks, and invited me to try one, which he did with gusto. I declined.

Albert's need for speed was also, admittedly combined with my incompetence, the cause of my Great Disaster of

Jenkin Road - yes, *Le Côte de Jenkin Road* of Tour de France fame, 2014. Anyone with the foggiest idea of what I'm talking about at this point, will know that Jenkin Road is probably the steepest hill in Sheffield, a very hilly city. Our round included descending Jenkin Road in our electric milk-float. On the fatal day, I was left about a hundred yards behind Albert who had raced off ahead. He shouted to me to 'bring it down'. I shouted back that I couldn't drive, but he insisted I 'bring it down'. Now, I was a callow youth who had only been inside a car on two or three occasions, but one thing I did know was that a car had three pedals, with the throttle on the right and the brake in the middle. I was unsure about the function of the third pedal on the left. This vehicle had only two pedals, a big fat one on the right and a small one on the left.

I fathomed out how to release the handbrake – I was a bright lad - and we set off down Jenkin Road at an increasing rate of knots, no matter how hard I pressed on the foot brake. In fact, it seemed to me that pressing the brake pedal was making us go even faster. I had reached quite a high speed before I took the risk of pressing the other pedal, just in case. The effect was instant, and the milk float screeched to a halt, dislodging half its load of milk and creating a mayhem of broken glass and a flood of creamy silver-top, not to mention our whole stock of Guernsey, half a crate. Albert was surprisingly calm and set about picking up the broken glass straightaway. Perhaps to him half a load of milk was a mere bagatelle, in view of the Bentley and the unlimited free supply of tomatoes at the sewage farm.

Then we drove back to the B&C depot and restocked. As on many occasions during my summer job stints, my face was red.

We milkmen were responsible for any losses through theft, miscalculation, leaving too many bottles of milk, or losing the takings, and the normal procedure regarding 'accidental breakages' was to present a broken bottle complete with its silver-foil cap intact as evidence, the loss being credited to the milkman's wages, but the Great Disaster was too much for the system to cope with, and the day's accounts were voided, to my relief. I wasn't sure how I would be able to pay for so much milk and had had visions of working the whole summer for nothing.

One or two of my partners had an interesting approach towards breakages. At a quiet point in the round, they would spend ten minutes or so fabricating accidental breakages by smashing a few empties and painstakingly fixing silver foil caps from a supply they carried in their pocket. This was a kind of revenge on the B&C and compensation for any unfair charges on their wages.

By far the most memorable days of my two summers' employment as a Co-op milkman were the ones I spent with placid, gentle, lovely Queenie. When I had to leave her at the end of the summer, it was like losing a dear old friend.

B&C Co-op Dairy horses. Queenie is on the right.

At the time I was working for B&C, the Co-op still had three Shire horses hauling milk wagons. I was lucky enough to spend two weeks working with one of them, an ageing mare with a beautiful temperament, called Queenie. The milkman I worked with, let's call him Wilf, was not the kindest of masters to Queenie. Whenever he came near to her head, she would flinch and rattle her hooves on the cobbles. As punishment for this reflex, Wilf would whack the old lady across the muzzle. I never remember her making a sound, apart from an occasional snuffle. Queenie had been working the same round for many years and moved through it six days a week like an automaton, stopping where she always stopped, then moving on to the next stopping place, and so on until home time and the haven of the dairy stables.

I am still nervous when near horses of any kind. They are massive, intimidating beasts and I find them unpredictable. Not to mention malodorous. For me, Queenie was the exception to the rule. After a few days, she stopped flinching whenever I came near and patted her neck. I needed her as a friend, even if she was a trifle smelly.

I learned from observing Wilf that the way to move Queenie forward was to shout 'Gooo on, Queenie!' and the way to stop her was to bellow 'Geh vay, Queenie!' She responded to no other instructions. For me the problem was that I was slower than the milkman's normal assistant, with the result that whenever I emerged from one of the passages leading to the backyard of several houses, Queenie had already moved on to the next halt, and I would have to chase after her to keep up.

One day towards the end of my fortnight with Queenie, Wilf did not turn up for work. I stood holding Queenie's reins, the wagon already fully loaded on a warm August morning in the dairy yard. Eventually, the gaffer came to me and told me that Wilf was not coming in that day and there was no replacement. Could I possibly take Queenie out on my own? He would come out personally later in the morning to give me a hand himself. He reassured me that all would be well, as Queenie knew the way off by heart and I would not get lost. He would see me safely across Attercliffe Road and then return to carry out his work at the dairy.

I was both terrified and elated. The emotional scars of the Jenkin Road catastrophe were still not healed, and I had never driven a horse and cart, let alone one laden with the Lord knows how many crates of milk!

I sweated blood that morning. We did the round at the gallop, but it was I who was galloping, not Queenie. She walked on at her customary measured pace, stopping at every halt on the round, in exactly the same place as every other day, for exactly the same amount of time. This meant, of course, that I was always chasing her, like some possessed madman, yelling the ridiculous mantra 'Geh vay, Queenie! Geh vay!'. No matter how many times I caught her up, grabbed her reins and asked her, first politely, then sternly, then desperately to 'stay here', Queenie would move on as soon as I had disappeared from view. She knew only one thing: once she had emerged from the dairy yard, she had to complete the round, and there was no stopping her. I was relieved of my duties late that morning, a broken man, exhausted, frustrated, and even more in awe than ever of the power and dignity of the Shire horse.

My days with Queenie were the best of times and the worst of times and remain amongst the fondest memories of my green youth.

Postscript

Here I come to the end of my musings about growing up in Sheffield. Was that all true? Is that how it really happened? Well, I have done my best to be truthful; this is how I saw things, what I thought, how I felt. Some of the experiences I have related in these pages remain as clear as day in my memory, in sharper focus than the events of last year, or maybe even last week. At least, I believe they do.

There are, as always with autobiographical writing, provisos and caveats, disclaimers and qualifications. Police experience has shown that if six people witness an incident, there will be six different accounts of what happened, often widely divergent. In history there is no such thing as a fact, no such thing as a truth; there are only interpretations, what our politicians now call 'spin'. These have been my facts; this has been my truth.

And if I could go back to January 1940, to the very fountainhead of my life in Heeley, if I could meet my fairy godmother and receive the customary three wishes, what would I ask for? I have given this some thought, and these are my three:

an automatic washing machine for Mum, a big, sunny back garden for Dad, with a greenhouse, and an unlimited supply of caseys for me.

Apart from that, mustn't grumble, it was reight enough.

John Foster, Sheffield, October, 2021

She saw . . . how life, far from being made up of little separate incidents which one lived one by one, became curled and whole like a wave which bore one up with it and threw one down with it, there, with a dash on the beach.

From *To the Lighthouse*, Virginia Woolf

Other books by John Foster

John Foster's books are available at www.johnfosterstories.com
and from Amazon sites worldwide
in paperback and Kindle version

You can contact the author at

johnfosterstories@gmail.com

◊

SCHOLAR'S MATE
a novel

jfs publications 2014
ISBN 978-0-9929459-0-9

Scholar's Mate tells the story of a little boy with an extraordinary gift, imprisoned alone in his silence, and of the quest for atonement and redemption of the man who deserted him in his hour of need. It is a tale of crime and detection, of murder and patricide, but also a moving story of love, friendship, courage and heroic sacrifice.

David York sets out, with the help of attractive private eye Lesley Bradshaw on a determined mission to unravel the dark secret buried deep in George Campbell's past, to unearth the roots of the trauma that has isolated him. His quest will take him across the world.

Stylishly crafted by the author of *Nine Times in Ten* and set in his native city of Sheffield, this gripping page-turner will not let you rest until you have read to the very end.
This is a novel that will make you smile but will also tear at your heart-strings.

◊

NINE TIMES IN TEN
stories short and long

Matador Press 2012
ISBN 9781780882666

"Nine times in ten the heart governs understanding."
Lord Chesterfield, Letters, 15th May 1749

"A kaleidoscope of 21 stories laced with humour, pathos, love, murder, drama and suspense, all with a common theme: the human condition."

Harry makes a Faustian pact in the world of professional football

Eight-year-old Robert finds the body of his murdered friend

Julie is transformed by a Roman love affair – will family ties frustrate her bid for freedom?

John consults a witch in Bogotá - will her predictions come true?

◊

FROM UNDER A BUSHEL
stories to chill your spine
stories to warm your heart

Indie publication 2019
ISBN: 9781074941314

"a scrumptious smörgasbord of stories to savour"

The Ilkhani of Gilan is a gently humorous account of the author's student days and his first involvement with the sport of kings.

A Streetcar to Argentina is a heart-warming coming of age story whose protagonists are an ill-assorted couple.

The Autograph Book is a love story spanning a lifetime, whilst the enigmatic *Mamma Mia* is set in the surgical ward of a Sheffield hospital.

On a more sinister note, *Baked Alaska* is a cautionary tale of ruthless and unbridled political ambition, and *Forgiveness*, based loosely on Greek myth, tells of a mother's craving for revenge.

The Ace of Spades is set in 1939 amongst the dying embers of the Spanish Civil War, whilst in *The Prayer* we witness a terrorist attack through the eyes of the young narrator.

Later editions include a ninth story, *Armageddon*, a companion piece to *The Ilkhani of Gilan*

◊

Open Heart Surgery
a slim volume of verse

Indie publication 2021
ISBN: 9798576925964

An eloquent, poignant and entertaining miscellany of verse, embracing humorous narrative poems, love poetry, and the author's reflections on life, personal, philosophical and polemic. Several poems are in Spanish.

◊

connect 5 brainstorm
lateral thinking puzzles for lively minds
Indie publication 2019
ISBN: 9781694016348

The puzzles
Each of these 260 lateral thinking puzzles has a solution which links all five clues.
Brainstorm until you find the connection.
Award yourself *four points* for the correct connection plus *one point* for solving each individual clue and a *bonus point* for solving all five.
So, the perfect answer scores *10 points*.

The Fun Way
As a group, with one appointed Questioner.
The Questioner can give hints as and when (s)he thinks fit.
Throw in your ideas and suggestions! Don't be shy! Brainstorm is the name of the game!

The Competitive Way
In teams, by turns, with preferably a neutral Questioner, or a (fair-minded) Questioner from the opposing team.

The Adventurous Way
Alone or with a partner, without a helpful Questioner. No sneaky looks at the answer! And don't give in too soon!

Example puzzle:
Question: What is the connection between Alistair and Johnny, Michael and Ralf, Bob and Mike, Vitali and Vladimir, and Rory and Tony?

See overleaf for answer

Answer to sample question:

They are pairs of sporting brothers, Brownlee (triathlon), Schuhmacher (Formula 1), Bryan (tennis), Klitschko (boxing), Underwood (rugby union).

Manufactured by Amazon.ca
Acheson, AB